The Ultimate Slow Cooker Cookbook!

The Best 130 Slow Cooker Recipes
in The World

BY

Stephanie Sharp

Warning - Disclaimer

The purpose of this book is to educate and entertain. The author and does not guarantee that anyone following these techniques, suggestions, tips, ideas, or strategies will become successful. The author shall have neither liability nor responsibility to anyone with respect to any loss or damage caused, or alleged to be caused, directly or indirectly by the information contained in this book.

Thank you so much for purchasing my book! As a reward for your purchase, you can now receive free books sent to you every day. All you have to do is just subscribe to the list by entering your email address in the box below and I will send you a notification every time I have a free promotion running. The books will absolutely be free with no work at all from you! Who doesn't want free books? No one! There are free and discounted books every day, and an email is sent to you 1-2 days beforehand to remind you so you don't miss out. It's that easy!

Just visit the link or scan QR-code to get started!

https://stephanie-sharp.subscribemenow.com

Table of Contents

Introduction

Are you looking for an easy and healthy way to cook your meals? Are you searching for a kitchen appliance that could take the pressure off you? Well, if that's the case then you should check out what we have prepared for you today.

We searched all over and we discovered that one of the most popular cooking methods these days is slow cooking. Slow cookers have become a must-have in the kitchen and millions of people all over the world opt for it each day.

Slow cookers allow you to cook healthy, delicious and rich dishes in a simple manner. Basically, all you have to do is to gather all your ingredients and the slow cooker will do the rest.

You don't have to be an expert in the kitchen to use a slow cooker. Just follow the directions and you will obtain the best dishes ever.

Purchase a slow cooker today and start cooking in a new and interesting way It might take you some time to get used to the slow cooker but once you do it will surprise you for sure.

Slow cooking is the best way to make incredible recipes for you and all your loved ones

If you've made the decision to use a slow cooker and you already have one, the next thing is to get your hands on a special slow cooker recipes collection.

That's where we can help you! We created the best slow cooker recipes collection ever,

The recipes you are about to discover are all so delicious and you have to try them all.

Get your own slow cooker cooking guide today and start this new culinary trip as soon as possible,

It will make you adore slow cookers in no time.

Trust us! It changed our vision about these appliances.

Have fun and enjoy your slow cooker!

Slow Cooker Recipes for Breakfast

Cooking in your slow cooker is truly an experience for a lifetime. Therefore, start your day with some of the best slow cooked breakfast recipes.

Strawberries Oatmeal

Just mix all the ingredients and enjoy a special breakfast!

Preparation time: 10 minutes

Cooking time: 8 hours

Servings: 6

Ingredients:

- 2 cups steel cut oats
- 2 cups almond milk
- 6 cups water
- 1 cup Greek yogurt
- 2 cups strawberries, chopped
- 1 teaspoon cinnamon powder
- 1 teaspoon vanilla extract

Method:

1. In your slow cooker, mix the oats with the almond milk, water, yogurt, 1 and ½ cups strawberries, cinnamon and the vanilla, toss, cover and cook on Low for 8 hours.

2. Divide the oatmeal into bowls, top each with the rest of the strawberries and serve.

Enjoy!

Nutrition: calories 200, fat 4, fiber 6, carbs 15, protein 6

Breakfast Potatoes and Sausage Mix

You've got to try this cheesy breakfast!

Preparation time: 10 minutes

Cooking time: 4 hours

Servings: 6

Ingredients:

- 3 gold potatoes, diced
- 1 red bell pepper, chopped
- 1 yellow onion, chopped
- 1 green bell pepper, chopped
- 12 ounces smoked chicken sausage, sliced
- 1 and ½ cups cheddar, shredded
- ½ cup sour cream
- ¼ teaspoon oregano, dried
- 10 ounces canned cream of chicken soup
- ¼ teaspoon basil, dried
- A pinch of salt and black pepper
- 2 tablespoons parsley, chopped

Method:

1. In your slow cooker, mix the potatoes with the red and green bell pepper, onion, sausage slices, sour cream, oregano, basil, salt, pepper and cream of chicken soup, toss, cover and cook on High for 4 hours.

2. Add the cheese and the parsley, leave everything aside for 10 minutes, divide between plates and serve for breakfast.

Enjoy!

Nutrition: calories 251, fat 4, fiber 7, carbs 20, protein 11

Slow Cooker Quinoa Bowls

This is so delicious and healthy! Try it today!

Preparation time: 10 minutes

Cooking time: 8 hours

Servings: 4

Ingredients:

- 2 cups water
- 1 cup coconut milk
- 1 cup quinoa
- 2 tablespoons maple syrup
- 2 tablespoons blackberries
- 1 tablespoon almonds, chopped

Method:

1. In your slow cooker, mix the quinoa with the water, milk and maple syrup, toss, cover and cook on Low for 8 hours.

2. Fluff the quinoa with a fork, divide it into bowls, top each with blackberries and almonds and serve for breakfast.

Enjoy!

Nutrition: calories 181, fat 3, fiber 6, carbs 20, protein 8

Hash Browns Breakfast

It's so rich and textured!

Preparation time: 10 minutes

Cooking time: 3 hours

Servings: 6

Ingredients:

- ¼ cup mushrooms, chopped
- ¼ cup yellow onion, chopped
- 3 tablespoons butter
- 3 tablespoons flour
- 1 cup milk
- ¼ teaspoon garlic powder
- A pinch of salt and black pepper
- ½ cup sour cream
- 20 ounces hash browns
- 1 cup cheddar cheese, shredded

Method:

1. Heat up a pan with the butter over medium heat, add the onion, mushrooms, garlic powder and flour, stir and cook for 3-4 minutes.

2. Add the milk, whisk well, cook for a couple more minutes, take off the heat and mix with the sour cream.

3. In your slow cooker, add the buttery mix, hash browns, salt, pepper and the cheese, toss, cover, cook on High for 3 hours, divide between plates and serve for breakfast.

Enjoy!

Nutrition: calories 251, fat 6, fiber 8, carbs 15, protein 8

Breakfast Casserole

It's a delicious breakfast idea!

Preparation time: 10 minutes

Cooking time: 5 hours

Servings: 6

Ingredients:

- 20 ounces frozen hash browns
- 8 bacon slices, cooked and chopped
- 6 green onions, chopped
- 8 ounces cheddar cheese, shredded
- ½ cup milk
- 12 eggs, whisked
- A pinch of salt and black pepper
- Cooking spray

Method:

1. Grease your slow cooker with the cooking spray, add hash browns, onions, bacon, salt and pepper and stir.

2. Add milk, eggs and the cheese, toss just a bit, cover, cook on Low for 5 hours, divide between plates and serve for breakfast.

Enjoy!

Nutrition: calories 265, fat 5, fiber 9, carbs 16, protein 9

Banana Breakfast Mix

It's sweet and tasty!

Preparation time: 10 minutes

Cooking time: 4 hours

Servings: 6

Ingredients:

- 1 stale French baguette, sliced
- ½ cup walnuts, chopped
- 4 ounces cream cheese
- 3 bananas, peeled and sliced
- 2 tablespoons brown sugar
- 3 eggs, whisked
- ¼ cup milk
- 1/3 cup honey
- 1 teaspoon cinnamon powder
- ½ tablespoons vanilla extract
- 2 tablespoons butter
- Cooking spray

Method:

1. Grease a slow cooker with the cooking spray and arrange baguette slices on the bottom.

2. Add cream cheese and spread.

3. Add walnuts, sugar and bananas over the cream cheese.

4. In a bowl, mix the eggs with the milk, honey, cinnamon, vanilla and the butter and whisk well.

5. Pour and spread this over the mix from the slow cooker, cover and cook on Low for 4 hours.

6. Divide between plates and serve for breakfast.

Enjoy!

Nutrition: calories 251, fat 6, fiber 7, carbs 16, protein 9

Zucchini Oatmeal

Try something different today!

Preparation time: 10 minutes

Cooking time: 8 hours

Servings: 4

Ingredients:

- 1 and ½ cups almond milk
- ½ cup steel cut oats
- 1 carrot, grated
- 1 zucchini, grated
- A pinch of nutmeg, ground
- A pinch of cloves, ground
- ½ teaspoon cinnamon powder
- 2 tablespoons brown sugar
- ¼ cup pecans, chopped

Method:

1. In your slow cooker, mix the oats with the milk, carrot, zucchini, nutmeg, cloves, sugar and cinnamon, toss, cover and cook on Low for 8 hours.

2. Divide into bowls, sprinkle pecans on top and serve for breakfast.

Enjoy!

Nutrition: calories 221, fat 6, fiber 8, carbs 16, protein 11

Monkey Bread

It's a special breakfast you can serve on a Sunday morning!

Preparation time: 10 minutes

Cooking time: 2 hours

Servings: 8

Ingredients:

- 10 cinnamon rolls dough
- 1 teaspoon cinnamon powder
- ¼ cup white sugar
- ½ cup brown sugar
- ½ cup butter, melted
- Cooking spray

Method:

1. Cut the cinnamon rolls in 6 pieces each and put them all in a bowl.

2. Add cinnamon, white and brown sugar and toss well.

3. Grease your slow cooker with cooking spray, add cinnamon rolls, also add the melted butter, toss, cover, cook on High for 2 hours, divide into bowls and serve for breakfast.

Enjoy!

Nutrition: calories 271, fat 9, fiber 7, carbs 20, protein 8

Turkey Sausage Casserole

It's an awesome combination!

Preparation time: 10 minutes

Cooking time: 4 hours

Servings: 8

Ingredients:

- 32 ounces tater tots
- 2 tablespoons heavy cream
- 6 eggs, whisked
- 1 pound turkey sausage, ground and cooked
- ½ teaspoon garlic powder
- ½ teaspoon thyme, dried
- A pinch of salt and black pepper
- 1 cups Colby Jack cheese, shredded
- Cooking spray

Method:

1. Grease a slow cooker with the cooking spray and add the tater tots on the bottom.

2. Add turkey sausage, garlic powder, thyme, salt and pepper.

3. Add the eggs mixed with the heavy cream and spread.

4. Add the cheese at the end, cover and cook on Low for 4 hours.

5. Divide between plates and serve.

Enjoy!

Nutrition: calories 271, fat 6, fiber 8, carbs 20, protein 15

Simple Cinnamon Rolls

This is a fast breakfast idea!

Preparation time: 10 minutes

Cooking time: 2 hours

Servings: 10

Ingredients:

- ¾ cup warm milk
- 2 and ½ teaspoons instant yeast
- ¼ cup sugar
- 3 tablespoons butter, melted
- 2 and ¾ cups flour
- 1 egg
- Cooking spray
- For the filling:
- 5 tablespoons butter, soft
- 1 tablespoon cinnamon powder
- 1/3 cup sugar

Method:

1. In a bowl, mix the milk with the years, ¼ cup sugar, 3 tablespoons butter, flour and the egg and stir until you obtain a dough.

2. Transfer this to a floured working surface and knead for 10 minutes.

3. In a bowl, mix 5 tablespoons butter with cinnamon and 1/3 cup sugar and blend using your mixer.

4. Roll the dough on the working surface and flatten it.

5. Spread the filling all over, roll well and cut into medium slices.

6. Grease a slow cooker with cooking spray, add cinnamon rolls inside, cover, cook on High for 2 hours, divide between plates and serve warm for breakfast.

Enjoy!

Nutrition: calories 221, fat 6, fiber 8, carbs 16, protein 8

Bacon Casserole

It's a culinary feast!

Preparation time: 10 minutes

Cooking time: 2 hours

Servings: 8

Ingredients:

- 2 leeks, sliced
- 5 bacon slices, cooked and chopped
- A pinch of salt and black pepper
- 6 eggs, whisked
- 2 teaspoons thyme, chopped
- 2 cups coconut cream
- 1 cup almond milk
- 1 tablespoon mustard
- ½ cup parsley, chopped
- Cooking spray

Method:

1. In a bowl, mix the eggs with thyme, salt, pepper coconut cream, milk, mustard, and parsley and whisk.

2. Grease your slow cooker with cooking spray, add the bacon and leeks on the bottom, add the eggs mix, spread, cover, cook on High for 2 hours, divide between plates and serve for breakfast.

Enjoy!

Nutrition: calories 200, fat 4, fiber 6, carbs 17, protein 8

Coconut Pear Bowls

It's the best way to start your day!

Preparation time: 10 minutes

Cooking time: 8 hours

Servings: 4

Ingredients:

- 6 pears, cored, peeled and cut into segments
- 2 tablespoons sunflower oil
- 6 ounces coconut milk
- 2/3 cup butter, melted
- 1 tablespoon vanilla extract
- 3 cups coconut, shredded
- ½ teaspoon cinnamon powder

Method:

1. In your slow cooker, mix the pears with the oil, milk, butter, vanilla, coconut and cinnamon, toss, cover, cook on Low for 8 hours, divide between plates and serve.

Enjoy!

Nutrition: calories 209, fat 4, fiber 4, carbs 17, protein 7

Bacon and Egg Casserole

This is so textured and flavored!

Preparation time: 10 minutes

Cooking time: 3 hours

Servings: 8

Ingredients:

- 20 ounces rice, cooked
- 8 bacon slices, cooked and chopped
- 1 red onion, chopped
- 12 eggs, whisked
- ½ cup milk
- A pinch of salt and black pepper
- Cooking spray

Method:

1. Grease your slow cooker with the cooking spray, spread the rice, bacon and onion on the bottom and toss a bit.

2. Add eggs, milk, salt and pepper, spread evenly, cover, cook on High for 3 hours, divide between plates and serve for breakfast.

Enjoy!

Nutrition: calories 233, fat 6, fiber 5, carbs 15, protein 8

Maple Pumpkin Oatmeal

This is so delicious and very easy to make if you have a slow cooker at hand!

Preparation time: 10 minutes

Cooking time: 8 hours

Servings: 2

Ingredients:

- Cooking spray
- ½ cup steel cut oats
- 2 cups milk
- 1 and ½ tablespoon maple syrup
- ½ teaspoon vanilla extract
- ½ teaspoon pumpkin pie spice
- ½ cup pumpkin flesh, mashed
- ¼ teaspoon cinnamon powder

Method:

1. In your slow cooker greased with the cooking spray, add the oats, milk, maple syrup, vanilla, pumpkin spice, pumpkin and cinnamon, cover, cook on Low for 8 hours, stir, divide into bowls and serve for breakfast.

Enjoy!

Nutrition: calories 272, fat 3, fiber 8, carbs 20, protein 11

Potato Frittata

It will amaze you with its taste!

Preparation time: 10 minutes

Cooking time: 6 hours

Servings: 4

Ingredients:

- Cooking spray
- 4 eggs, whisked
- 1 cup red potatoes, chopped
- 1 cup milk
- 1 cup ham, chopped
- Salt and black pepper to the taste

Method:

1. In a bowl, mix the eggs with potatoes, milk, ham, salt and pepper and whisk.

2. Grease your slow cooker with cooking spray, add the potato mixture, spread, cover, cook on Low for 6 hours, slice, divide between plates and serve.

Enjoy!

Nutrition: calories 260, fat 8, fiber 6, carbs 18, protein 9

Veggie Frittata

Sometimes, a veggie frittata is all you need!

Preparation time: 10 minutes

Cooking time: 4 hours

Servings: 2

Ingredients:

- Cooking spray
- ½ red onion, chopped
- ½ red bell pepper, chopped
- 2 tablespoons tomatoes, chopped
- 1 ounce canned green chili pepper, chopped
- ½ teaspoon oregano, dried
- 1 teaspoon milk
- Salt and black pepper to the taste
- 3 ounces cheddar cheese, shredded
- 4 eggs, whisked

Method:

1. Grease your slow cooker with cooking spray, add the onion, bell pepper, sun dried tomatoes and green chilies and toss.

2. In a bowl, mix eggs with skim milk, salt and pepper.

3. Add eggs mixed with salt, pepper and the milk, spread, sprinkle the cheese all over, cover, cook on Low for 4 hours, divide between plates and serve for breakfast.

Enjoy!

Nutrition: calories 274, fat 4, fiber 7, carbs 18, protein 16

Tofu Casserole

Try a vegan slow cooked dish for a change!

Preparation time: 10 minutes

Cooking time: 4 hours

Servings: 4

Ingredients:

- 1 teaspoon lime zest, grated
- 14 ounces tofu, cubed
- 1 tablespoon lime juice
- 1 tablespoon apple cider vinegar
- 1 tablespoon avocado oil
- 2 garlic cloves, minced
- 10 ounces spinach, torn
- ½ cup yellow onion, chopped
- ½ teaspoon basil, dried
- 8 ounces mushrooms, sliced
- Salt and black pepper to the taste
- ¼ teaspoon red pepper flakes
- Cooking spray

Method:

1. Spray your slow cooker with cooking spray, arrange tofu cubes on the bottom, add lime zest, lime juice, vinegar, oil, garlic, onion, basil, mushrooms, salt, pepper and pepper flakes, cover and cook on Low for 3 hours and 30 minutes.

2. Add the spinach, toss a bit, cover, cook on Low for 30 minutes more, divide between plates and serve.

Enjoy!

Nutrition: calories 226, fat 6, fiber 8, carbs 17, protein 8

Blackberries Oatmeal

This is very delicious!

Preparation time: 10 minutes

Cooking time: 8 hours

Servings: 4

Ingredients:

- 1 cup blackberries
- 1 cup steel cut oats
- 1 cup milk
- 2 tablespoons brown sugar
- ½ teaspoon vanilla extract
- Cooking spray

Method:

1. Grease your slow cooker with cooking spray, add oats, milk, sugar, blackberries and vanilla, cover, cook on Low for 8 hours, stir, divide into bowls and serve for breakfast.

Enjoy!

Nutrition: calories 202, fat 6, fiber 8, carbs 11, protein 7

Cinnamon Pumpkin Butter

It's original and so tasty!

Preparation time: 10 minutes

Cooking time: 5 hours

Servings: 8

Ingredients:

- 30 ounces pumpkin puree
- 2 teaspoons cinnamon powder
- 1 and ¼ cups maple syrup
- 1 teaspoon vanilla extract
- 1 teaspoon ginger powder
- ½ teaspoon nutmeg, ground

Method:

1. In your slow cooker, mix pumpkin with maple syrup, vanilla, ginger, cinnamon and nutmeg, stir, cover, cook on High for 5 hours, divide into jars and serve for breakfast.

Enjoy!

Creamy Coconut Oatmeal

Here's what you can eat today!

Preparation time: 10 minutes

Cooking time: 8 hours

Servings: 8

Ingredients:

- 8 cups water
- 2 cups steel cut oats
- 10 ounces coconut milk
- 2 tablespoons white sugar
- 1 teaspoon vanilla extract

Method:

1. In your slow cooker, mix the water with the oats, milk, sugar and vanilla, cover, cook on Low for 8 hours, stir, divide into bowls and serve for breakfast.

Enjoy!

Slow Cooker Lunch Recipes

Make something really delicious for lunch today. Just gather all the ingredients you need and prepare a tassty and rich lunch recipe! Check out what we have prepared for you today.

Chicken Soup

It's tasty and so delicious!

Preparation time: 10 minutes

Cooking time: 6 hours and 15 minutes

Servings: 6

Ingredients:

- 2 carrots, chopped
- 1 and ½ pounds chicken breast, boneless and skinless
- 3 celery stalks, chopped
- 1 yellow onion, chopped
- 3 garlic cloves, minced
- 6 cups chicken stock
- 1 cup water
- 2 bay leaves
- 1 teaspoons Italian seasoning
- 2 cups cheese tortellini
- 1 tablespoon parsley, chopped
- Salt and black pepper

Method:

1. In your slow cooker, mix the carrots with the chicken, celery, onion, garlic, stock, water, bay leaves, Italian seasoning, salt and pepper, toss, cover and cook on Low for 6 hours.

2. Add the tortellini, cover and cook on Low for 15 minutes more.

3. Shred the meat, divide it into bowls, ladle the soup, sprinkle the parsley on top and serve.

Enjoy!

Nutrition: calories 271, fat 7, fiber 9, carbs 17, protein 9

Lentils Soup

This is perfect for your lunch!

Preparation time: 10 minutes

Cooking time: 6 hours

Servings: 6

Ingredients:

- 1 yellow onion, chopped
- 5 carrots, chopped
- 1 yellow bell pepper, chopped
- 4 garlic cloves, minced
- 3 cups red lentils
- Salt and black pepper to the taste
- 4 cups chicken stock
- 3 cups water
- Juice of 1 lemon
- Zest of 1 lemon, grated
- 1 tablespoon rosemary, chopped

Method:

1. In a slow cooker, mix the onion with the carrots, bell pepper, garlic, lentils, water and stock, toss, cover and cook on Low for 6 hours.

2. Add salt, pepper, lemon juice, lemon zest and the rosemary, toss, ladle into bowls and serve.

Enjoy!

Nutrition: calories 281, fat 14, fiber 8, carbs 20, protein 16

Mexican Soup

It's very delicious and spicy! Try it now!

Preparation time: 10 minutes

Cooking time: 8 hours and 10 minutes

Servings: 6

Ingredients:

- 1 yellow onion, chopped
- 1 and ½ tablespoons coconut oil, melted
- 4 red bell peppers, chopped
- 2 pounds beef meat, ground
- 3 tablespoons chili powder
- 2 tablespoons cumin, ground
- 1 teaspoon sweet paprika
- Salt and black pepper to the taste
- ½ teaspoon garlic powder
- ½ teaspoon onion powder
- 1 teaspoon cinnamon powder
- 28 ounces canned tomatoes, chopped
- 25 ounces bone broth
- 8 ounces canned green chilies, chopped
- 5 ounces coconut milk

Method:

1. Heat up a pan with the oil over medium heat, add the bell peppers and the onions, stir and cook for 5 minutes.

2. Add the meat, stir, cook for 5 minutes more, drain excess grease and transfer this to your slow cooker.

3. Also add chili powder, cumin, paprika, salt, pepper, garlic powder, onion powder, cinnamon, tomatoes, broth, green chilies and the coconut milk, toss, cover and cook on Low for 8 hours.

4. Divide the soup into bowls and serve for lunch.

Enjoy!

Nutrition: calories 301, fat 8, fiber 8, carbs 20, protein 17

Chicken and Rice Soup

It's a tasty combination of ingredients!

Preparation time: 10 minutes

Cooking time: 7 hours

Servings: 6

Ingredients:

- 1 pound chicken breasts, skinless and boneless
- 1 tablespoon olive oil
- 1 cup wild rice
- 1 cup butternut squash, cubed
- 1 sweet potato, cubed
- 1 apple, cored, peeled and cubed
- 1 zucchini, chopped
- 1 yellow onion, chopped
- ¼ cup of red curry paste
- 1 tablespoon ginger, grated
- 4 garlic cloves, minced
- 3 tablespoons fish sauce
- 2 tablespoons soy sauce
- A pinch of salt and black pepper
- 1 tablespoon basil, dried
- 1 teaspoon cumin, ground
- 27 ounces coconut milk
- 5 cups chicken stock
- 1 tablespoon cornstarch
- ¼ cup water
- 2 tablespoons brown sugar
- 2 tablespoons lime juice

- 1/3 cup peanut butter, soft

Method:

1. In your slow cooker, mix the oil with the chicken, rice, squash, sweet potato, apple, zucchini, onion, curry paste, ginger, garlic, sugar, fish sauce, soy sauce, salt, pepper, basil, cumin and stock, toss, cover and cook on Low for 6 hours and 30 minutes.

2. Add cornstarch mixed with water, coconut milk, lime juice and peanut butter, stir, cover, cook on Low for 30 minutes more, divide into bowls and serve for lunch.

Enjoy!

Nutrition: calories 288, fat 6, fiber 9, carbs 20, protein 18

Thai Chicken Soup

It's a special lunch idea you just have to try!

Preparation time: 10 minutes

Cooking time: 4 hours

Servings: 7

Ingredients:

- 1 tablespoon brown sugar
- 2 tablespoons red curry paste
- 2 tablespoons cilantro, chopped
- 2 garlic cloves, minced
- 1 red bell pepper, chopped
- 2 tablespoons ginger, grated
- 1 yellow onion, chopped
- 1 red chili, chopped
- 12 ounces coconut milk
- 4 cups chicken stock
- 1 and ½ pounds chicken breasts, boneless, skinless and cubed
- 1 cup peas
- 7 ounces rice noodles
- Juice of 1 lime
- Zest of 1 lime, grated
- 2 tablespoons fish sauce
- A pinch of salt

Method:

1. In your food processor, mix the sugar with the curry paste, cilantro, garlic, bell pepper, ginger, onion and chili and pulse well.

2. Transfer this to your slow cooker, add the stock, coconut milk, chicken and a pinch of salt, toss, cover and cook on High for 3 hours and 30 minutes.

3. Add lime juice, lime zest, fish sauce, rice noodles and the peas, toss, cover, cook on High for 30 minutes more, divide into bowls and serve.

Enjoy!

Nutrition: calories 300, fat 7, fiber 9, carbs 20, protein 16

Mushroom and Tortellini Soup

This creamy white soup tastes amazing!

Preparation time: 10 minutes

Cooking time: 3 hours

Servings: 6

Ingredients:

- 16 ounces baby spinach
- 2/3 cup yellow onion, chopped
- 3 tablespoons butter
- 3 garlic cloves, minced
- A pinch of salt and black pepper
- 5 cups veggie stock
- 1 and ½ cups half and half
- ½ teaspoon Italian seasoning
- 2 teaspoons garlic powder
- ¼ teaspoon thyme, dried
- 15 ounces cheese tortellini
- 3 cups mushrooms, sliced
- ½ cup parmesan, grated

Method:

1. Heat up a pan with the butter over medium heat, add the mushrooms, onion and the garlic, stir and cook for 2-3 minutes.

2. Add the spinach, salt and pepper, toss and transfer this to your slow cooker.

3. Add the stock, half and half, Italian seasoning, garlic powder and thyme, toss, cover and cook on High for 2 hours and 30 minutes.

4. Add the tortellini and the parmesan, toss, cover, cook on High for 30 minutes more, divide into bowls and serve.

Enjoy!

Nutrition: calories 237, fat 8, fiber 9, carbs 20, protein 14

Chicken and Veggies Soup

This is so hearty!

Preparation time: 10 minutes

Cooking time: 6 hours

Servings: 6

Ingredients:

- 2 chicken breasts, skinless and boneless
- 1 cup peas
- 1 cup corn
- 1 cup carrots, chopped
- 2 potatoes, chopped
- 1 celery stalk, chopped
- 1 yellow onion, chopped
- 4 ounces cream cheese
- 4 cups chicken stock
- 1 tablespoon chicken bouillon
- 4 cups heavy cream
- 2 teaspoons garlic powder
- Salt and black pepper to the taste
- 1 tube biscuit dough

Method:

1. In your slow cooker, mix the chicken with the corn, peas, celery, carrots, onions, potatoes, stock, cream cheese, garlic powder and chicken bouillon, toss, cover and cook on Low for 5 hours and 30 minutes.

2. Add heavy cream, salt and pepper, toss, cover, cook on Low for 30 minutes more, ladle into bowls and serve.

Enjoy!

Nutrition: calories 311, fat 7, fiber 12, carbs 20, protein 17

Black Beans Soup

This is a good idea for lunch! Why don't you try it today?

Preparation time: 10 minutes

Cooking time: 6 hours

Servings: 6

Ingredients:

- 1 yellow onion, chopped
- 2 garlic cloves, minced
- 2 carrots, chopped
- 2 celery stalks, chopped
- 1 pound black beans, dried
- 1 cup salsa
- 1 tablespoon chili powder
- 1 teaspoon oregano, dried
- ½ tablespoon cumin, ground
- 4 cups veggie stock
- 2 cups water

Method:

1. In your slow cooker, mix the onion with the garlic, carrots, celery, black beans, salsa, chili powder, oregano, cumin, stock and the water, toss, cover and cook on Low for 6 hours.

2. Blend the soup using an immersion blender, divide into bowls and serve.

Enjoy!

Nutrition: calories 299, fat 7, fiber 9, carbs 20, protein 17

Cauliflower Cream

You'll love this!

Preparation time: 10 minutes

Cooking time: 8 hours

Servings: 6

Ingredients:

- 2 cups cauliflower florets, chopped
- 3 cups broccoli florets, chopped
- 2 garlic cloves, minced
- ½ cup shallot, chopped
- 3 and ½ cups veggie stock
- 1 carrot, chopped
- Salt and black pepper to the taste
- 1 cup milk
- 6 ounces cheddar cheese, shredded
- 1 cup Greek yogurt

Method:

1. In your slow cooker, mix the cauliflower with the broccoli, garlic, shallot, stock, carrot, salt, pepper and milk, toss, cover and cook on Low for 7 hours and 30 minutes.

2. Add the cheese and the yogurt, toss, divide into bowls and serve for lunch.

Enjoy!

Nutrition: calories 300, fat 7, fiber 9, carbs 22, protein 19

Squash Soup

Here's another creamy and rich soup!

Preparation time: 10 minutes

Cooking time: 4 hours

Servings: 6

Ingredients:

- 2 garlic cloves, minced
- 1 carrot, chopped
- 2 cups veggie stock
- 1 apple, cored and chopped
- 1 butternut squash, peeled and cubed
- 1 sage spring
- 1 yellow onion, chopped
- A pinch of salt and white pepper
- A pinch of nutmeg, ground
- A pinch of cinnamon powder
- ½ cup coconut milk

Method:

1. In your slow cooker, mix the garlic with the carrot, stock, apple, squash. Sage, onion, salt, pepper, nutmeg, cinnamon and the milk, toss, cover and cook on High for 4 hours.

2. Blend the soup using an immersion blender, ladle the soup into bowls and serve.

Enjoy!

Nutrition: calories 271, fat 8, fiber 9, carbs 29, protein 18

Special Beef Stew

It's a special beef stew we love!

Preparation time: 10 minutes

Cooking time: 8 hours and 10 minutes

Servings: 6

Ingredients:

- 2 pounds beef chuck, cut into cubes
- Salt and black pepper to the taste
- 1 teaspoon sweet paprika
- 1/3 cup white flour
- 3 tablespoons olive oil
- 1 pound white potatoes, cubed
- ½ pound mushrooms, sliced
- 3 carrots, chopped
- 1 yellow onion, chopped
- 2 tablespoons tomato paste
- 2 cups beef stock
- 3 thyme springs, chopped
- 1 teaspoon caraway seeds
- ½ cup parsley, chopped

Method:

1. Heat up a pan with the oil over medium high heat, add the meat dredged in flour, toss, brown for 3-4 minutes and transfer to your slow cooker.

2. Heat up the pan again over medium heat, add the onion, carrots, mushrooms, salt and pepper, stir, cook for 4-5 minutes more and also transfer to your slow cooker.

3. Add the paprika, potatoes, tomato paste, stock, caraway seeds and thyme, toss, cover and cook on Low for 8 hours.

4. Add the parsley, stir, divide into bowls and serve.

Enjoy!

Nutrition: calories 299, fat 7, fiber 9, carbs 29, protein 17

Turkey Stew

This is so healthy and easy to make at home!

Preparation time: 10 minutes

Cooking time: 6 hours

Servings: 4

Ingredients:

- 4 turkey thighs, skinless and bone-in
- 1 teaspoon allspice, ground
- Salt and black pepper to the taste
- ½ butternut squash, cubed
- 30 ounces canned chickpeas, drained and rinsed
- 27 ounces canned tomatoes, chopped
- 1 cup apricots, dried
- ½ cup gold raisins
- 8 carrots, sliced
- 3 red onions, chopped
- 2 red chilies, dried and crushed
- Juice of ½ lemon
- 2 cups cilantro, chopped
- 1 cup parsley, chopped

Method:

1. In your slow cooker, mix the turkey thighs with the allspice, salt, pepper, squash, chickpeas, tomatoes, apricots, carrots, raisins, onions and red chilies, cover and then cook on High for about 6 hours.

2. In your blender, mix the cilantro with the parsley, lemon juice, salt and pepper and pulse really well.

3. Divide the turkey stew into bowls, top each serving with the pesto you've made and serve for lunch.

Enjoy!

Nutrition: calories 310, fat 7, fiber 9, carbs 26, protein 17

Beef Chili

Try a delicious chili for lunch today!

Preparation time: 10 minutes

Cooking time: 8 hours

Servings: 4

Ingredients:

- ½ cup brewed coffee
- ¼ cup tomato paste
- 2 pounds beef chuck, cubed
- 1 tablespoon chili powder
- Salt and black pepper to the taste
- 30 ounces canned pinto beans, drained and rinsed
- ½ cup tortilla chips, crushed
- 4 cups white rice, cooked
- Cheddar cheese, shredded for serving

Method:

1. In your slow cooker, mix the coffee with the tomato paste, beef cubes, chili powder, salt, pepper and pinto beans, cover and cook on Low for 8 hours.

2. Stir the chili, divide it between plates, add the rice next to it and serve with crushed tortilla chips and cheddar cheese on top.

Enjoy!

Nutrition: calories 267, fat 8, fiber 8, carbs 25, protein 16

Pork and Veggie Stew

This tender stew is awesome!

Preparation time: 10 minutes

Cooking time: 8 hours

Servings: 4

Ingredients:

- 1 pound potatoes, cubed
- 3 carrots, chopped
- 2 celery stalks, chopped
- 3 garlic cloves, minced
- 1 tablespoon ginger, grated
- 1/3 cup white flour
- Salt and black pepper to the taste
- 2 pounds pork shoulder, cubed
- 3 bay leaves
- 2 cups water
- ½ teaspoon allspice, ground
- 1 teaspoon thyme, dried
- 15 ounces canned tomatoes, chopped

Method:

1. In your slow cooker, mix the potatoes with the carrots, celery, garlic, ginger, flour, salt, pepper, pork, bay leaves, water, allspice, thyme and tomatoes, toss, cover and cook on Low for 8 hours.

2. Discard bay leaves, divide into bowls and serve for lunch.

Enjoy!

Nutrition: calories 300, fat 6, fiber 8, carbs 26, protein 20

Exotic Stew

Here's a delicious Caribbean lunch idea!

Preparation time: 10 minutes

Cooking time: 7 hours

Servings: 4

Ingredients:

- 1/3 cup white flour
- ¼ teaspoon allspice, ground
- Salt and black pepper to the taste
- 3 thyme springs
- 2 pound beef stew meat, cubed
- 1 pound gold potatoes, cubed
- 3 carrots, chopped
- 1-inch ginger, grated
- 2 teaspoons Worcestershire sauce
- 1 garlic clove, minced
- 10 ounces canned tomatoes and chilies, chopped
- 4 scallions, chopped

Method:

1. In your slow cooker, mix the beef with the flour, allspice, salt, pepper, thyme, potatoes, carrots, ginger, Worcestershire sauce, garlic and tomatoes, toss, cover and cook on Low for 7 hours.

2. Divide the stew into bowls and serve with scallions sprinkled on top.

Enjoy!

Nutrition: calories 318, fat 8, fiber 9, carbs 18, protein 17

Seafood Stew

This seafood stew is incredible!

Preparation time: 10 minutes

Cooking time: 3 hours and 30 minutes

Servings: 2

Ingredients:

- 1 garlic clove, minced
- 12 ounces canned tomatoes, chopped
- ½ pound sweet potatoes, peeled and cubed
- 2 cups chicken stock
- ½ small yellow onion, chopped
- ½ teaspoon cilantro, dried
- ½ teaspoon thyme, dried
- ½ teaspoon basil, dried
- A pinch of salt and black pepper
- 1 pound mixed scallops and peeled and deveined shrimp

Method:

1. In your slow cooker, mix the garlic with the sweet potatoes, tomatoes, onion, thyme, cilantro, basil, salt, pepper and the stock, cover and cook on High for 3 hours.

2. Add scallops and the shrimp, cover, cook on High for 30 minutes more, divide into bowls and serve for lunch.

Enjoy!

Nutrition: calories 230, fat 3, fiber 5, carbs 17, protein 7

Lamb Stew

You will adore this special lunch dish!

Preparation time: 10 minutes

Cooking time: 8 hours

Servings: 2

Ingredients:

- 1 pound lamb meat, cubed
- 2 tablespoons white flour
- Salt and black pepper to the taste
- 1 tablespoon olive oil
- ½ teaspoon rosemary, dried
- 1 small onion, sliced
- ¼ teaspoon thyme, dried
- 1 cup water
- ½ cup baby carrots
- 1 cup gold potatoes, cubed

Method:

1. Heat up a pan with the oil over medium-high heat, add the meat dredged in the flour, brown it on all sides and transfer to your slow cooker.

2. Add onion, salt, pepper, rosemary, thyme, water, carrots and sweet potatoes, stir, cover, cook on Low for 8 hours, divide into bowls and serve.

Enjoy!

Nutrition: calories 350, fat 8, fiber 3, carbs 20, protein 18

Chickpeas and Turkey Stew

Even your kids will love this dish!

Preparation time: 10 minutes

Cooking time: 8 hours and 10 minutes

Servings: 2

Ingredients:

- ½ pound turkey, ground
- ½ tablespoon olive oil
- 1 small yellow onion, chopped
- 1 garlic clove, minced
- 1 tablespoon poblano pepper, chopped
- ¼ cup celery, chopped
- ¼ cup carrots, chopped
- 6 ounces canned tomatoes, chopped
- 6 ounces canned chickpeas, drained
- ½ cup veggie stock
- ½ teaspoon turmeric powder
- ½ teaspoon sweet paprika
- ½ teaspoon coriander, ground
- ½ tablespoon parsley, chopped
- Salt and black pepper to the taste

Method:

1. Heat up a pan with the oil over medium-high heat, add turkey, onion and garlic, stir, brown for 10 minutes and transfer to your slow cooker.

2. Add poblano, celery, carrots, tomatoes, chickpeas, stock, turmeric, paprika, coriander, parsley, salt and pepper, cover, cook on Low for 8 hours, stir, divide into bowls and serve for lunch.

Enjoy!

Nutrition: calories 462, fat 7, fiber 9, carbs 30, protein 20

Easy Veggie Gumbo

You've got to try this today!

Preparation time: 10 minutes

Cooking time: 8 hours

Servings: 4

Ingredients:

- 1 tablespoon olive oil
- ½ green bell pepper, chopped
- ½ yellow onion, chopped
- ½ celery stalks, chopped
- 1 garlic cloves, minced
- 6 ounces canned tomatoes, chopped
- 1 cup veggie stock
- Salt and black pepper to the taste
- 4 ounces white mushrooms, sliced
- 4 ounces canned kidney beans, drained
- 1 small zucchini, chopped

Method:

1. In your slow cooker, mix the oil with bell pepper, onion, celery, garlic, tomatoes, stock, mushrooms, beans, zucchini, salt and pepper, stir, cover, cook on Low for 8 hours, divide into bowls and serve for lunch.

Enjoy!

Nutrition: calories 242, fat 4, fiber 7, carbs 14, protein 11

Italian Eggplant Stew

Here's a flavored Italian style stew!

Preparation time: 10 minutes

Cooking time: 4 hours

Servings: 4

Ingredients:

- 20 ounces canned tomatoes, chopped
- 2 red onions, chopped
- 2 red bell peppers, chopped
- 2 eggplants, cubed
- ½ tablespoon sweet paprika
- 1 teaspoon cumin, ground
- Salt and black pepper to the taste
- Juice of ½ lime
- ½ tablespoon cilantro, chopped

Method:

1. In your slow cooker, mix the tomatoes with the onions, bell peppers, eggplants, paprika, cumin, salt, pepper and lime juice, toss, cover and cook on High for 4 hours.

2. Divide the stew into bowls, sprinkle the cilantro on top and serve for lunch.

Enjoy!

Nutrition: calories 241, fat 4, fiber 6, carbs 12, protein 9

Slow Cooker Side Dish Recipes

Do you have any idea how delicious slow cooked side dishes are? Well, we know! That's why we gathered the best ones for you. Try them all.

Hash Browns Side Dish

This is so easy to make!

Preparation time: 10 minutes

Cooking time: 3 hours

Servings: 12

Ingredients:

- 2 pounds hash brown potatoes
- 10 ounces condensed cream of chicken soup
- 1 cup cheddar cheese, shredded
- 1 and ½ cups milk
- Salt and black pepper to the taste
- ½ cup butter, melted
- ¼ cup yellow onion, chopped
- ¾ cup cornflakes, crushed

Method:

1. In your slow cooker, mix the hash browns with the cream of chicken soup, cheese, milk, salt, pepper, butter and the onion, cover and cook on Low for 3 hours.

2. Add the cornflakes, toss, divide between plates and serve as a side dish.

Enjoy!

Nutrition: calories 251, fat 6, fiber 9, carbs 17, protein 9

Easy Broccoli Mix

This is both delicious and healthy!

Preparation time: 10 minutes

Cooking time: 3 hours

Servings: 10

Ingredients:

- 6 cups broccoli florets, chopped
- 10 ounces condensed cream of celery soup
- 1 and ½ cups cheddar cheese, shredded
- 2 tablespoons butter
- Salt and black pepper to the taste
- ½ teaspoon Worcestershire sauce
- 1 cup butter crackers, crushed
- ¼ cup yellow onion, chopped

Method:

1. In your slow cooker, mix the broccoli with cream of celery, onion, 1 cup cheese, salt, pepper and Worcestershire sauce and toss.

2. Sprinkle the crackers on top, cover and cook on High for 2 hours and 50 minutes.

3. Add the rest of the cheese, cover, cook on High for 10 minutes more, divide between plates and serve as a side dish.

Enjoy!

Nutrition: calories 181, fat 11, fiber 5, carbs 11, protein 6

Bean Mix

This is so colored and tasty!

Preparation time: 10 minutes

Cooking time: 6 hours

Servings: 10

Ingredients:

- 1 and ½ cups tomato paste
- 2 celery ribs, chopped
- 1 green bell pepper, chopped
- 1 yellow onion, chopped
- A pinch of salt and black pepper
- 15 ounces canned kidney beans, drained
- 15 ounces canned black eyed peas, drained
- ½ cup water
- ½ cup brown sugar
- ½ cup Italian salad dressing
- 15 ounces canned great northern beans, drained
- 14 ounces canned corn, drained
- 15 ounces canned lima beans, drained
- 15 ounces canned black beans, drained
- 1 tablespoon cider vinegar
- 2 bay leaves
- 1 teaspoon ground mustard

Method:

1. In your slow cooker, mix the tomato paste with the celery, bell pepper, onion, kidney beans, black eyed peas, northern beans, corn, lima beans, black beans, vinegar, mustard, bay leaves, water, sugar, salt, pepper and Italian salad dressing, toss, cover and cook on Low for 6 hours.

2. Divide between plates and serve as a side dish.

Enjoy!

Nutrition: calories 255, fat 4, fiber 7, carbs 20, protein 8

Simple Green Beans

This is so fresh and delightful!

Preparation time: 10 minutes

Cooking time: 2 hours

Servings: 12

Ingredients:

- 16 cups French-style green beans
- ½ cup brown sugar
- ½ cup butter, melted
- A pinch of salt and black pepper
- 1 teaspoon soy sauce

Method:

1. In your slow cooker, mix the beans with sugar, butter, salt, pepper and the soy sauce, cover, cook on Low for 2 hours, toss, divide between plates and serve as a side dish.

Enjoy!

Nutrition: calories 151, fat 7, fiber 4, carbs 17, protein 2

Creamy Corn Mix

This is a creamy and rich side dish!

Preparation time: 10 minutes

Cooking time: 4 hours

Servings: 20

Ingredients:

- 10 cups corn
- 21 ounces cream cheese, cubed
- A pinch of salt and white pepper
- ¼ cup sugar
- ½ cup milk
- ½ cup heavy cream
- 4 bacon strips, cooked and crumbed
- 2 tablespoons green onions, chopped
- ½ cup butter, melted

Method:

1. In your slow cooker, mix the corn with the cream cheese, salt, pepper, sugar, milk, cream and melted butter, cover and cook on Low for 4 hours.

2. Divide the mix between plates, sprinkle the bacon and the green onions on top and serve as a side dish.

Enjoy!

Nutrition: calories 251, fat 20, fiber 5, carbs 17, protein 5

Peas and Carrots Mix

It's a buttery side dish you have to try soon!

Preparation time: 10 minutes

Cooking time: 5 hours

Servings: 12

Ingredients:

- 1 yellow onion, chopped
- 1 pound carrots, sliced
- ¼ cup water
- ¼ cup butter, melted
- ¼ cup honey
- A pinch of salt and black pepper
- 4 garlic cloves, minced
- 15 ounces peas

Method:

1. In your slow cooker, mix the onion with the carrots, water, butter, honey, salt, pepper, garlic and the peas, cover and cook on Low for 5 hours.

2. Stir the mix, divide between plates and serve as a side dish.

Enjoy!

Nutrition: calories 161, fat 6, fiber 4, carbs 15, protein 3

Simple Pilaf

This goes so well with a steak!

Preparation time: 10 minutes

Cooking time: 3 hours

Servings: 6

Ingredients:

- 1 cup white rice
- 2 garlic cloves, minced
- ¼ cup butter, melted
- 6 green onions, chopped
- ½ pound white mushrooms, sliced
- 2 cups beef stock

Method:

1. Heat up a pan with the butter over medium heat, add the rice, sauté for a couple of minutes and transfer to your slow cooker.

2. Add green onions, garlic, mushrooms and the stock, cover, cook on Low for 3 hours, divide between plates and serve as a side dish.

Enjoy!

Nutrition: calories 211, fat 8, fiber 3, carbs 20, protein 5

Glazed Carrots

This is easy to make but it's so full of intense flavors!

Preparation time: 10 minutes

Cooking time: 6 hours

Servings: 6

Ingredients:

- ½ cup peach preserves
- 2 pound baby carrots
- ½ cup butter, melted
- ¼ cup brown sugar
- ½ teaspoon cinnamon powder
- 1 teaspoon vanilla extract
- A pinch of nutmeg, ground
- 2 tablespoons water
- 2 tablespoons cornstarch

Method:

1. In your slow cooker, mix the carrots with peach preserves, butter, sugar, cinnamon, vanilla and nutmeg and toss.

2. Add cornstarch mixed with the water, toss, cover and cook on Low for 6 hours.

3. Divide between plates and serve as a side dish.

Enjoy!

Nutrition: calories 271, fat 12, fiber 6, carbs 20, protein 3

Creamy Potatoes

This is exactly what we need today!

Preparation time: 10 minutes

Cooking time: 7 hours

Servings: 10

Ingredients:

- 2 and ½ pounds red potatoes, cubed
- 6 bacon strips, cooked and chopped
- 9 ounces cream cheese, soft
- 10 ounces condensed cream of potato soup
- 1 envelope ranch salad dressing
- 3 tablespoons green onions, sliced
- ¼ cup milk

Method:

1. Put the potatoes in your slow cooker, add cream cheese, cream of potato soup, ranch dressing, onions and the milk, toss, cover and cook on Low for 7 hours.

2. Divide the mix between plates, sprinkle the bacon on top and serve as a side dish.

Enjoy!

Nutrition: calories 251, fat 12, fiber 4, carbs 20, protein 6

Squash Side Dish

It's really fresh and tender!

Preparation time: 10 minutes

Cooking time: 5 hours

Servings: 12

Ingredients:

- 1 butternut squash, cubed
- 1 cup whole grain brown and rice mix
- 1 yellow onion, chopped
- ½ cup water
- 2 teaspoons thyme, chopped
- 3 garlic cloves, minced
- 14 ounces veggie stock
- A pinch of salt and black pepper
- 6 ounces baby spinach

Method:

1. In your slow cooker, mix the squash with the grains, onion, water, thyme, garlic, salt, pepper, spinach and the stock, cover, cook on Low for 5 hours, stir, divide between plates and serve as a side dish.

Enjoy!

Nutrition: calories 100, fat 2, fiber 3, carbs 20, protein 6

Simple Mushroom Mix

You only need a few ingredients to make this side dish!

Preparation time: 10 minutes

Cooking time: 4 hours

Servings: 6

Ingredients:

- 1 yellow onion, chopped
- 1 pound mushrooms, halved
- ½ cup butter, melted
- 1 envelope Italian salad dressing

Method:

1. In your slow cooker, mix the onion with the mushrooms, butter and Italian salad dressing, toss, cover, cook on Low for 4 hours, divide between plates and serve as a side dish.

Enjoy!

Nutrition: calories 100, fat 7, fiber 2, carbs 7, protein 6

Green Beans and Potatoes

This is one of our favorite side dishes!

Preparation time: 10 minutes

Cooking time: 7 hours

Servings: 10

Ingredients:

- 8 bacon strips, cooked and chopped
- 5 gold potatoes, cubed
- 1 and ½ pounds green beans
- 1 yellow onion, chopped
- ¼ cup chicken stock
- A pinch of salt and black pepper

Method:

1. In your slow cooker, mix the potatoes with the green beans, onion, stock, salt and pepper, cover and cook on Low for 7 hours.

2. Stir, divide between plates, sprinkle the bacon on top and serve.

Enjoy!

Nutrition: calories 116, fat 5, fiber 4, carbs 16, protein 6

Spinach and Rice

It's the best thing you can cook today!

Preparation time: 10 minutes

Cooking time: 3 hours

Servings: 8

Ingredients:

- 2 tablespoons butter, melted
- 8 ounces cream cheese, soft
- A pinch of salt and black pepper
- 1 yellow onion, chopped
- ¼ teaspoon thyme, dried
- 2 cups white rice
- 2 cups cheddar cheese, shredded
- 4 cups chicken stock
- 20 ounces spinach, chopped
- ½ cup bread crumbs
- ¼ cup parmesan, grated

Method:

1. In your slow cooker, mix the butter with the onion, cream cheese, salt, pepper, thyme, rice and stock, toss, cover and cook on Low for 3 hours.

2. Add the spinach, breadcrumbs and the parmesan, toss, cover, cook on Low for 30 minutes more, divide between plates and serve as a side dish.

Enjoy!

Nutrition: calories 271, fat 8, fiber 6, carbs 20, protein 15

Delicious Sweet Potato Mix

These taste divine!

Preparation time: 10 minutes

Cooking time: 5 hours

Servings: 12

Ingredients:

- 4 pounds sweet potatoes, cubed
- 1 cup walnuts, chopped
- ½ cup brown sugar
- ½ cup dried cherries, chopped
- ¼ cup apple juice
- ½ cup maple syrup

Method:

1. In your slow cooker, mix the potatoes with the walnuts, sugar, cherries, apple juice and maple syrup, cover and cook on Low for 5 hours.

2. Stir, divide between plates and serve as a side dish.

Enjoy!

Nutrition: calories 261, fat 6, fiber 7, carbs 28, protein 7

Shredded Sweet Potatoes

The flavor is perfect and the taste is impressive!

Preparation time: 10 minutes

Cooking time: 4 hours and 10 minutes

Servings: 10

Ingredients:

- 1 yellow onion, chopped
- 2 tablespoons olive oil
- 2 shallots, chopped
- ¼ cup parsley, chopped
- A pinch of salt and black pepper
- 2 teaspoons chipotle pepper, ground
- 3 pounds sweet potatoes, shredded
- 2 cups Monterey Jack cheese, shredded
- 8 ounces cream cheese
- 15 ounces apple wood smoked bacon, cooked and crumbed
- ½ teaspoon sweet paprika

Method:

1. Heat up a pan with the oil over medium high heat, add the onion and shallots, toss, sauté for 7 minutes and transfer to your slow cooker.

2. Add chipotle pepper, potatoes, cheese, cream cheese, paprika, salt and pepper, toss, cover and cook on Low for 4 hours.

3. Add the parsley and the bacon, toss, divide between plates and serve as a side dish.

Enjoy!

Nutrition: calories 261, fat 12, fiber 8, carbs 20, protein 18

Orange Sweet Potatoes

This citrus flavored side dish is special!

Preparation time: 10 minutes

Cooking time: 6 hours

Servings: 8

Ingredients:

- 4 pounds sweet potatoes, peeled and sliced
- ½ cup orange juice
- 3 tablespoons brown sugar
- A pinch of salt and black pepper
- ½ teaspoon thyme, chopped
- ½ teaspoon sage, dried

Method:

1. In your slow cooker, mix potato slices with salt, pepper sugar, orange juice, thyme and sage, cover, cook on Low for 6 hours, divide between plates and serve as a side dish.

Enjoy!

Nutrition: calories 162, fat 4, fiber 7, carbs 17, protein 6

Orange Carrots and Parsnips

This root veggie mix is delicious!

Preparation time: 10 minutes

Cooking time: 4 hours

Servings: 6

Ingredients:

- 2 pounds carrots, cut into chunks
- 2 tablespoons orange zest, grated
- 1 pounds parsnips, cut into chunks
- 1 cup orange juice
- 1 cup chicken stock
- A pinch of salt and black pepper
- ¼ cup cilantro, chopped
- 1 tablespoon avocado oil

Method:

1. In your slow cooker, mix the carrots with the parsnips, orange zest, orange juice, stock, salt, pepper, oil and the cilantro, toss, cover, cook on High for 4 hours, divide between plates and serve as a side dish.

Enjoy!

Nutrition: calories 180, fat 4, fiber 6, carbs 11, protein 6

Balsamic Brussels Sprouts

It's one of the best side dish ideas!

Preparation time: 10 minutes

Cooking time: 4 hours

Servings: 6

Ingredients:

- 2 tablespoons white sugar
- ½ cup balsamic vinegar
- 2 tablespoons sunflower oil
- 2 pounds Brussels sprouts, halved
- A pinch of salt and black pepper
- 2 tablespoons cilantro, chopped

Method:

1. In your slow cooker, mix the sprouts with the sugar, vinegar, oil, salt, pepper and the cilantro, toss, cover, cook on Low for 4 hours, divide between plates and serve as a side dish.

Enjoy!

Nutrition: calories 158, fat 5, fiber 6, carbs 13, protein 6

Easy Sprouts and Pine Nuts Mix

It's a special and rich combination!

Preparation time: 10 minutes

Cooking time: 3 hours

Servings: 4

Ingredients:

- 2 pounds Brussels sprouts, halved
- 2 cups veggie stock
- A pinch of salt and black pepper
- 2 tablespoons balsamic vinegar
- 2 tablespoons avocado oil
- ¼ cup pine nuts, toasted
- 2 tablespoons parsley, chopped

Method:

1. In your slow cooker, mix the sprouts with the stock, salt, pepper, vinegar, oil, pine nuts and parsley, toss, cover, cook on High for 3 hours, divide between plates and serve as a side dish.

Enjoy!

Nutrition: calories 149, fat 4, fiber 4, carbs 8, protein 6

Rosemary Brussels Sprouts

The rosemary gives such a special flavor to this side dish!

Preparation time: 10 minutes

Cooking time: 3 hours

Servings: 10

Ingredients:

- 1 cup red onion, cut into wedges
- 2 pounds Brussels sprouts, halved
- A pinch of salt and black pepper
- 1 cup apple juice
- 3 tablespoons olive oil
- 2 tablespoons rosemary, chopped

Method:

1. In your slow cooker, mix the sprouts with the onion, salt, pepper, apple juice, oil and the rosemary, toss, cover, cook on High for 3 hours, divide between plates and serve as a side dish.

Enjoy!

Nutrition: calories 140, fat 4, fiber 4, carbs 11, protein 6

Slow Cooker Appetizer Recipes

Get ready for your next party with these next appetizer recipes! You'll see how amazing these are! Try them all and enjoy!

Carrot Pate

Don't miss out on this special appetizer! Try it right away!

Preparation time: 10 minutes

Cooking time: 5 hours

Servings: 8

Ingredients:

- 16 ounces carrots, chopped
- 2 garlic cloves, minced
- 1 tablespoon ginger, grated
- ½ teaspoon cinnamon powder
- A pinch of salt and black pepper
- 2 tablespoons lime juice
- ½ teaspoon smoked paprika
- 3 tablespoons olive oil
- ¼ cup veggie stock

Method:

1. In your slow cooker, mix the carrots with the garlic, paprika, ginger, cinnamon, salt, pepper, lime juice, oil and the stock, cover and cook on Low for 5 hours.

2. Transfer this to your blender, pulse well, divide into bowls and serve as an appetizer.

Enjoy!

Nutrition: calories 200, fat 3, fiber 7, carbs 15, protein 8

Broccoli Spread

You will love this!

Preparation time: 10 minutes

Cooking time: 2 hours

Servings: 8

Ingredients:

- 1 sweet onion, chopped
- 2 garlic cloves, minced
- ¼ teaspoon red pepper flakes, crushed
- 4 cups broccoli florets, chopped
- 8 ounces sour cream
- 1 tablespoon scallions, chopped
- ½ cup mayonnaise
- ½ cup milk
- A pinch of salt and black pepper

Method:

1. In your slow cooker, mix the sweet onion with garlic, pepper flakes, broccoli, sour cream, scallions, mayo, milk, salt and pepper, stir, cover, cook on Low for 2 hours, blend using an immersion blender, divide into bowls and serve.

Enjoy!

Nutrition: calories 201, fat 14, fiber 8, carbs 8, protein 6

Artichoke Dip

Trust us! This is so tasty!

Preparation time: 10 minutes

Cooking time: 2 hours

Servings: 12

Ingredients:

- 10 ounces spinach, chopped
- 8 ounces sour cream
- ½ cup artichoke hearts, chopped
- ½ cup sun-dried tomatoes, chopped
- ¼ cup yellow onion, chopped
- 1 garlic clove, minced

Method:

1. In your slow cooker, mix the spinach with the artichokes, cream, tomatoes, onion and the garlic, toss, cover, cook on Low for 2 hours, whisk well again, divide into bowls and serve as a party dip.

Enjoy!

Nutrition: calories 181, fat 4, fiber 9, carbs 15, protein 7

Cauliflower Spread

This is what you need for your next party!

Preparation time: 10 minutes

Cooking time: 7 hours

Servings: 4

Ingredients:

- 2 cups cauliflower florets
- ½ cup cashews, soaked overnight and drained
- 2 cups milk
- 1 teaspoon garlic powder
- ¼ teaspoon sweet paprika

Method:

1. In your slow cooker, mix the cauliflower with the cashews, milk, garlic powder and the paprika, cover, cook on Low for 7 hours, blend using an immersion blender, divide into bowls and serve as a dip.

Enjoy!

Nutrition: calories 181, fat 7, fiber 4, carbs 14, protein 6

Peppers Dip

This is the best party dip ever!

Preparation time: 10 minutes

Cooking time: 5 hours

Servings: 8

Ingredients:

- 2 cups chicken stock
- 6 big red bell peppers, deseeded
- Salt and black pepper to the taste
- 2 garlic cloves, minced
- 3 tablespoons olive oil
- ½ cup lime juice
- 1 cup tahini

Method:

1. In your slow cooker, mix the peppers with the stock, salt and pepper, cover, cook on Low for 5 hours, drain, transfer the bell peppers to your blender, add the garlic, oil, lime juice and tahini, pulse well, divide into bowls and serve as an appetizer.

Enjoy!

Nutrition: calories 200, fat 4, fiber 2, carbs 14, protein 6

Mussels Appetizer Salad

This seafood appetizer is the best!

Preparation time: 10 minutes

Cooking time: 2 hours and 30 minutes

Ingredients:

- 1 pound mussels
- ½ cup chicken stock
- 3 tablespoons lemon juice
- ½ cup olive oil
- 1 garlic clove, minced
- 2 handfuls mixed salad greens
- 1 avocado, pitted, peeled and cubed
- 1 red bell pepper, cut into thin strips

Method:

1. In your slow cooker, mix the mussels with the stock and lemon juice, cover, cook on Low for 2 hours and 30 minutes, drain the mussels, transfer them to a salad bowl, add the oil, the garlic, salad greens, avocado and bell pepper, toss and serve as an appetizer.

Enjoy!

Nutrition: calories 205, fat 4, fiber 4, carbs 15, protein 5

Olives Salsa

This looks so great!

Preparation time: 10 minutes

Cooking time: 2 hours

Servings: 3

Ingredients:

- 1 cup black olives, pitted
- 1 cup kalamata olives, pitted
- 1 cup green olives, pitted
- 5 garlic cloves, minced
- Salt and black pepper to the taste
- 2 tablespoons olive oil
- ½ cup veggie stock
- 1 teaspoon Italian seasoning
- 1 teaspoon lemon zest, grated

Method:

1. In your slow cooker, mix the black olives with the green ones and the kalamata ones, add the garlic, salt, pepper, oil, stock, seasoning and lemon zest, toss, cover, cook on Low for 2 hours, divide into bowls and serve as an appetizer.

Enjoy!

Nutrition: calories 180, fat 2, fiber 2, carbs 14, protein 7

Cheesy Cauliflower Florets

Serve this appetizer for your guests and they will love it!

Preparation time: 10 minutes

Cooking time: 4 hours

Servings: 2

Ingredients:

- 1 cauliflower head, florets separated
- Salt and black pepper to the taste
- ½ cup cheddar cheese, shredded
- 2 tablespoons chicken stock
- 1 tablespoon chives, chopped
- ½ teaspoon onion powder
- 2 tablespoons olive oil

Method:

1. In your slow cooker, combine the cauliflower florets with salt, pepper, stock, chives, onion powder and the oil, cover, cook on Low for 4 hours, add the cheese and leave aside for 10 minutes more.

2. Divide into bowls and serve as an appetizer.

Enjoy!

Nutrition: calories 180, fat 6, fiber 7, carbs 17, protein 6

Crab Spread

You have never tried such an appetizer!

Preparation time: 10 minutes

Cooking time: 1 hour and 20 minutes

Servings: 2

Ingredients:

- 2 ounces crabmeat
- 1 teaspoon lime juice
- 2 tablespoons parmesan, grated
- 2 green onions, chopped
- 2 ounces canned artichokes hearts, drained and chopped
- 2 ounces cream cheese, soft
- A drizzle of olive oil

Method:

1. In your slow cooker, mix the crabmeat with the lime juice, parmesan, onions, artichokes, cream cheese and the oil, toss, cover, cook on Low for 1 hour and 20 minutes, whisk well, divide into bowls and serve as an appetizer.

Enjoy!

Nutrition: calories 161, fat 3, fiber 2, carbs 13, protein 5

White Beans Spread

It's really delicious!

Preparation time: 10 minutes

Cooking time: 7 hours

Servings: 4

Ingredients:

- ½ cup white beans, dried
- 4 tablespoons cashews, soaked for 12 hours and blended
- 1 teaspoon apple cider vinegar
- 1 cup veggie stock

Method:

1. In your slow cooker, mix the beans with the cashews, vinegar and stock, cover, cook on Low for 7 hours, blend using an immersion blender, divide into bowls and serve.

Enjoy!

Nutrition: calories 191, fat 6, fiber 5, carbs 14, protein 7

Greek Spinach Dip

This Mediterranean appetizer is incredible!

Preparation time: 10 minutes

Cooking time: 1 hour

Servings: 2

Ingredients:

- 2 tablespoons sour cream
- ½ cup Greek yogurt
- 5 ounces spinach
- 4 ounces water chestnuts, chopped
- 1 garlic clove, minced
- Salt and black pepper to the taste

Method:

1. In your slow cooker, the sour cream with the yogurt, spinach, chestnuts, garlic, salt and pepper, cover, cook on High for 1 hour, blend using an immersion blender, divide into bowls and serve.

Enjoy!

Nutrition: calories 191, fat 5, fiber 7, carbs 15, protein 6

Mushroom Salsa

Try this salsa as soon as possible!

Preparation time: 10 minutes

Cooking time: 4 hours

Servings: 2

Ingredients:

- 1 cup red bell peppers, chopped
- 1 small yellow onion, chopped
- 1 garlic clove, minced
- ½ pound mushrooms, cubed
- 12 ounces tomato sauce
- ¼ cup cheddar, shredded
- Salt and black pepper to the taste

Method:

1. In your slow cooker, mix the mushrooms with bell peppers, onion, garlic, tomato sauce, salt and pepper, stir, cover, cook on Low for 4 hours, divide into bowls, sprinkle the cheese on top and serve as an appetizer.

Enjoy!

Nutrition: calories 195, fat 4, fiber 7, carbs 12, protein 5

Chickpeas Salsa

It's different and really special!

Preparation time: 10 minutes

Cooking time: 10 hours

Servings: 2

Ingredients:

- 1 cup chickpeas
- 2 cups veggie stock
- 1 red onion, chopped
- ¼ tablespoon ginger, grated
- 4 garlic cloves, minced
- 2 Thai peppers, chopped
- ¼ tablespoons cumin, ground
- ¼ tablespoons coriander, ground
- ¼ tablespoons red chili powder
- ¼ tablespoons garam masala
- ¼ tablespoon tamarind paste
- 1 tablespoon cilantro, chopped
- 1 tablespoon lime juice

Method:

1. In a blender, mix the ginger with the garlic, Thai peppers, cumin, coriander, chili powder, garam masala, tamarind paste and lime juice, pulse well and transfer to your slow cooker.

2. Also add the chickpeas, onion and the stock, cover, cook on Low for 10 hours, divide into bowls, sprinkle the cilantro on top and serve.

Enjoy!

Nutrition: calories 355, fat 5, fiber 14, carbs 16, protein 11

Beans Tacos

These Mexican tacos are so incredible!

Preparation time: 10 minutes

Cooking time: 6 hours

Servings: 2

Ingredients:

- 13 ounces canned pinto beans, drained
- ¼ cup chili sauce
- 2 ounces chipotle pepper in adobo sauce, chopped
- ½ cup corn
- 2 ounces tomato paste
- ½ tablespoon cocoa powder
- ¼ teaspoon cinnamon powder
- 4 taco shells

Method:

1. In your slow cooker, mix the beans with the chili sauce, chipotle pepper, corn, tomato paste, cocoa powder and cinnamon, cover, cook on Low for 6 hours, toss, divide into the taco shells and serve as an appetizer.

Enjoy!

Nutrition: calories 262, fat 3, fiber 6, carbs 20, protein 17

Buttery Onion Dip

This onion dip is really different from anything you have tried in the past!

Preparation time: 10 minutes

Cooking time: 8 hours

Servings: 2

Ingredients:

- 1 and ½ cups yellow onions, chopped
- A pinch of salt and black pepper
- 1 tablespoon avocado oil
- ½ tablespoon butter
- ½ cup milk
- 2 tablespoons mayonnaise

Method:

1. In your slow cooker, mix the onions with salt, pepper, oil and the butter, cover and cook on Low for 7 hours.

2. Transfer the onions to a blender, add the mayo and the milk, pulse well, divide into bowls and serve as an appetizer.

Enjoy!

Nutrition: calories 190, fat 4, fiber 4, carbs 19, protein 5

Lemony Lentils Spread

This lemony spread is what you should serve at your next party!

Preparation time: 10 minutes

Cooking time: 6 hours

Servings: 2

Ingredients:

- 1 small yellow bell pepper, chopped
- 1 small yellow onion, chopped
- 2 carrots, chopped
- 2 garlic cloves, minced
- 1 cup chicken stock
- 1 and ½ cups red lentils, dried
- Salt and black pepper to the taste
- ½ tablespoon rosemary, chopped
- 1 tablespoon lemon zest, grated
- 1 tablespoon lemon juice

Method:

1. In your slow cooker, mix the bell pepper with the onion, carrots, garlic, stock, lentils, salt, pepper, rosemary, lemon zest and lemon juice, cover, cook on Low for 6 hours, blend using an immersion blender, divide into bowls and serve as an appetizer.

Enjoy!

Nutrition: calories 220, fat 2, fiber 5, carbs 18, protein 6

Cod Sticks

Even the most pretentious guests will love this!

Preparation time: 10 minutes

Cooking time: 2 hours

Servings: 2

Ingredients:

- 1 eggs, whisked
- ½ pound cod fillets, cut into medium strips
- ½ cup flour
- Salt and black pepper to the taste
- A drizzle of olive oil

Method:

1. In a bowl, mix flour with salt and pepper and stir.

2. Put the egg in another bowl and whisk it.

3. Dip fish sticks in the egg, then dredge them in flour mix, arrange all the sticks in your slow cooker greased with the oil, cover, cook on High for 2 hours, arrange on a platter and serve as an appetizer.

Enjoy!

Nutrition: calories 210, fat 3, fiber 4, carbs 14, protein 9

Squid Bowls

This tastes really great!

Preparation time: 10 minutes

Cooking time: 7 hours

Servings: 2

Ingredients:

- ½ pound squid, cleaned and cut into rings
- 1 tablespoon sugar
- 1 small ginger piece, grated
- 2 garlic cloves, minced
- 1 tablespoon soy sauce
- 1 cup veggie stock
- 1 leek stalks, chopped

Method:

1. In your slow cooker, mix the squid rings with the sugar, ginger, garlic, stock, leek and soy sauce, cover, cook on Low for 7 hours, toss, divide into bowls and serve as an appetizer.

Enjoy!

Nutrition: calories 210, fat 6, fiber 4, carbs 14, protein 6

Apple Spread

It's one of our favorite spreads!

Preparation time: 10 minutes

Cooking time: 8 hours

Servings: 2

Ingredients:

- 2 cups apples, peeled, cored and chopped
- ¼ teaspoon allspice, ground
- ¼ teaspoon ginger powder
- 1 tablespoon lemon juice
- 2 teaspoons cinnamon powder
- ¼ teaspoon nutmeg, ground
- ½ cup water
- 2 tablespoons maple syrup

Method:

1. In your slow cooker, mix the apples with the allspice, ginger, lemon juice, cinnamon, nutmeg, water and maple syrup, cover, cook on Low for 8 hours, blend using an immersion blender, divide into bowls and serve.

Enjoy!

Nutrition: calories 190, fat 4, fiber 6, carbs 16, protein 7

Sausage Bites

They look incredible!

Preparation time: 10 minutes

Cooking time: 4 hours

Servings: 2

Ingredients:

- 6 mini smoked sausages
- 2 tablespoons tomato sauce
- 1 teaspoon sweet paprika
- ½ cup grape juice

Method:

1. In your slow cooker, the sausages with the tomato sauce, paprika and the grape juice, cover, cook on Low for 4 hours, toss, divide into bowls and serve as an appetizer.

Enjoy!

Nutrition: calories 271, fat 4, fiber 6, carbs 17, protein 9

Slow Cooker Main Dish Recipes

This is really one of the best culinary experiences of your life! Enjoy these next amazing, rich and delicious slow cooked dishes! They are really special! See for yourself!

Salmon and Broccoli

This could be your dinner!

Preparation time: 10 minutes

Cooking time: 3 hours

Servings: 2

Ingredients:

- 2 medium salmon fillets, boneless
- Salt and black pepper to the taste
- 2 tablespoons soy sauce
- 2 tablespoons maple syrup
- 16 ounces broccoli florets
- 2 tablespoons lemon juice

Method:

1. Put the broccoli in your slow cooker, add the salmon fillets on top, also add soy sauce, salt, pepper maple syrup and lemon juice, cover, cook on Low for 3 hours, divide between plates and serve.

Enjoy!

Nutrition: calories 260, fat 7, fiber 2, carbs 20, protein 8

Delicious Tuna Bites

This is exactly what you need today!

Preparation time: 10 minutes

Cooking time: 2 hours

Servings: 2

Ingredients:

- ½ pound tuna loin, cubed
- 1 garlic clove, minced
- 4 jalapeno peppers, chopped
- 1 cup olive oil
- 3 red chili peppers, chopped
- 2 teaspoons black peppercorns, ground
- Salt and black pepper to the taste

Method:

1. In your slow cooker, mix the tuna with the garlic, jalapenos, oil, chili peppers, peppercorns, salt and pepper, cover, cook on Low for 2 hours, divide between plates and serve with a side salad.

Enjoy!

Nutrition: calories 270, fat 4, fiber 6, carbs 19, protein 8

Clam Bowls

This is so easy to make!

Preparation time: 10 minutes

Cooking time: 4 hours

Servings: 2

Ingredients:

- 10 ounces clams
- ¼ cup coconut milk
- 1 tablespoon olive oil
- 1 green bell pepper, chopped
- 1 yellow onion, chopped
- Salt and black pepper to the taste

Method:

1. In your slow cooker, mix the clams with the oil, milk, bell pepper, onion, salt and pepper, cover, cook on Low for 4 hours, divide into bowls and serve.

Enjoy!

Nutrition: calories 270, fat 4, fiber 7, carbs 17, protein 7

Fast Gumbo

Try this magnificent gumbo today!

Preparation time: 10 minutes

Cooking time: 6 hours

Servings: 2

Ingredients:

- ½ pound chicken breast, skinless, boneless and cubed
- ½ pound smoked sausage, sliced
- ½ pound shrimp, peeled and deveined
- ½ yellow onion, chopped
- ½ green bell pepper, chopped
- ½ jalapeno, chopped
- Salt and black pepper to the taste
- 1 celery rib, chopped
- 12 ounces canned tomatoes, chopped
- 1 and ½ teaspoon garlic, minced
- 1 cup chicken stock
- ½ teaspoon oregano, dried

Method:

1. In your slow cooker, mix the chicken with the sausage, onion, bell pepper, jalapeno, salt, pepper, celery, tomatoes garlic, stock and the oregano, cover and cook on Low for 5 hours and 30 minutes.

2. Add the shrimp, cover, cook on Low for 30 minutes more, divide into bowls and serve.

Enjoy!

Nutrition: calories 351, fat 6, fiber 8, carbs 20, protein 8

Tomato Shrimp Mix

It's perfect for a Sunday meal!

Preparation time: 10 minutes

Cooking time: 1 hour

Servings: 4

Ingredients:

- 3 tablespoons olive oil
- 2 pounds shrimp, peeled and deveined
- 2 teaspoons garlic, minced
- 1 cup tomato sauce
- Salt and black pepper

Method:

1. In your slow cooker, mix the oil with the shrimp, garlic, tomato sauce, salt and pepper, toss, cover, cook on Low for 1 hour, divide between plates and serve.

Enjoy!

Nutrition: calories 220, fat 6, fiber 6, carbs 18, protein 11

Shrimp and Parsley Mix

The parsley gives the shrimp such an amazing taste!

Preparation time: 10 minutes

Cooking time: 1 hour and 30 minutes

Servings: 4

Ingredients:

- 2 tablespoons olive oil
- ¼ cup chicken stock
- 1 tablespoon garlic, minced
- 2 tablespoons parsley, chopped
- Juice of 1 lime
- 1 pound shrimp, peeled and deveined
- A pinch of salt and black pepper

Method:

1. In your slow cooker, mix the oil with the stock, garlic, parsley, lime juice, salt and pepper and whisk.

2. Add the shrimp, cover, cook on Low for 1 hour and 30 minutes, toss, divide between plates and serve.

Enjoy!

Nutrition: calories 223, fat 4, fiber 7, carbs 16, protein 16

Tomato Shrimp and Asparagus

This is perfect for a fancy dinner!

Preparation time: 10 minutes

Cooking time: 1 hour and 30 minutes

Servings: 4

Ingredients:

- 1 teaspoon olive oil
- 5 ounces tomato sauce
- 1 pound shrimp, peeled and deveined
- 1 bunch asparagus spears, trimmed
- ½ tablespoon Italian seasoning

Method:

1. In your slow cooker, mix the oil with the tomato sauce, shrimp, asparagus and seasoning, toss, cover, cook on Low for 1 hour and 30 minutes, divide between plates and serve.

Enjoy!

Nutrition: calories 212, fat 2, fiber 3, carbs 17, protein 11

Herbed Shrimp

The herbs used for this dish are divine!

Preparation time: 10 minutes

Cooking time: 1 hour and 30 minutes

Servings: 4

Ingredients:

- 1 pound shrimp, peeled and deveined
- 2 tablespoons avocado oil
- 1 garlic clove, minced
- 1 tablespoon oregano, chopped
- 1 tablespoon cilantro, chopped
- 10 ounces canned tomatoes, chopped

Method:

1. In your slow cooker, mix the shrimp with the oil, garlic, oregano, cilantro and the tomatoes, cover, cook on Low for 1 hour and 30 minutes, divide between plates and serve.

Enjoy!

Nutrition: calories 232, fat 5, fiber 6, carbs 18, protein 12

Gingery Fish Curry

This Indian dish is really good!

Preparation time: 10 minutes

Cooking time: 3 hours

Servings: 4

Ingredients:

- 1/3 cup olive oil
- 2 hot chilies, chopped
- 1 yellow onion, chopped
- 2 garlic cloves, minced
- 1 teaspoon ginger, grated
- 2 teaspoons coriander, ground
- 1 tablespoon cumin, ground
- 2 teaspoons mustard seeds
- 2 teaspoons turmeric powder
- 2 pounds white fish fillets, cut into medium chunks
- 3 tablespoons cilantro, chopped

Method:

1. In your slow cooker, mix the oil with the chilies, onion, garlic, ginger, coriander, cumin, mustard seeds and turmeric and whisk.

2. Add the fish, cover, cook on Low for 3 hours, divide into bowls, sprinkle the cilantro on top and serve.

Enjoy!

Nutrition: calories 261, fat 6, fiber 8, carbs 20, protein 11

Cod and Orange Sauce

It's the perfect fish with the perfect sauce!

Preparation time: 10 minutes

Cooking time: 2 hours and 30 minutes

Servings: 4

Ingredients:

- 4 green onions, chopped
- 1 teaspoon ginger, grated
- 1 tablespoon olive oil
- 4 cod fillets, boneless and skinless
- Juice of 1 orange
- Zest of 1 orange, grated
- A pinch of salt and black pepper
- 1 cup veggie stock

Method:

1. In your slow cooker, mix the onions with the ginger, oil, orange juice, orange zest, stock, salt and pepper and whisk.

2. Add the fish, toss it gently, cover, cook on Low for 2 hours and 30 minutes, divide everything between plates and serve.

Enjoy!

Nutrition: calories 261, fat 3, fiber 2, carbs 18, protein 8

Chicken Breasts Stuffed with Spinach

It's light and tasty!

Preparation time: 10 minutes

Cooking time: 6 hours

Servings: 4

Ingredients:

- 4 chicken breasts, skinless, boneless
- 1 tablespoon olive oil
- 1 small yellow onion, chopped
- 1 small red bell pepper, chopped
- 2 teaspoons garlic, minced
- 6 ounces spinach
- 1 tablespoon lime juice
- 1 cup chicken stock
- A pinch of salt and black pepper
- A handful cilantro, chopped

Method:

1. In a bowl, mix the onion with the bell pepper, garlic, spinach, salt and pepper, toss, cut a pocket in each chicken breast and stuff them with the spinach mix.

2. Add the oil to your slow cooker, add stuffed chicken, lime juice and the stock, cover, cook on Low for 6 hours, divide between plates, sprinkle the cilantro on top and serve.

Enjoy!

Nutrition: calories 271, fat 4, fiber 3, carbs 22, protein 17

Chicken Meatballs

These are perfect for a casual dinner party!

Preparation time: 2 hours

Cooking time: 4 hours

Servings: 12

Ingredients:

- 2 cups chicken, ground
- A pinch of salt and black pepper
- 2 green onions, chopped
- 2 celery stalks, chopped
- 1 egg, whisked
- 2 garlic cloves, minced
- 1 tablespoon parsley, chopped
- 1 cup tomato sauce
- 2 tablespoons olive oil

Method:

1. In a bowl, mix the chicken with salt, pepper, green onions, celery, garlic, parsley, salt, pepper and egg, stir well and shape medium meatballs.

2. Grease your slow cooker with the oil, add the meatballs, also add the tomato sauce, cover, cook on High for 4 hours, divide between plates and serve.

Enjoy!

Nutrition: calories 270, fat 7, fiber 2, carbs 16, protein 17

Chicken and Mushrooms

This slow cooked main dish is so amazing!

Preparation time: 10 minutes

Cooking time: 6 hours

Servings: 4

Ingredients:

- 3 pounds chicken thighs, skinless and boneless
- 2 tablespoons olive oil
- 1 yellow onion, chopped
- 1 and ½ teaspoons basil, dried
- ¼ cup tomato sauce
- 3 garlic cloves, minced
- 6 ounces canned tomatoes, chopped
- ½ cup chicken stock
- 2 pounds white mushrooms, sliced

Method:

1. Heat up a pan with the oil over medium-high heat, add the chicken, brown on all sides, transfer to your slow cooker, add onion, basil, tomato sauce, garlic, tomatoes, stock and the mushrooms, cover, cook on Low for 6 hours, divide between plates and serve.

Enjoy!

Nutrition: calories 281, fat 4, fiber 6, carbs 20, protein 16

Chicken and Salsa Mix

It's so nice to try something different each day! Here's today suggestion!

Preparation time: 10 minutes

Cooking time: 7 hours

Servings: 4

Ingredients:

- 4 chicken breasts, boneless and skinless
- 15 ounces salsa
- 1/3 cup chicken stock
- 1 teaspoon onion powder
- 1 teaspoon garlic powder
- ½ tablespoon cilantro, dried
- ½ tablespoon oregano, dried
- ½ teaspoon sweet paprika
- Salt and black pepper to the taste
- ½ teaspoon cumin, ground
- 1 teaspoon chili powder
- 2 tablespoons parsley, chopped

Method:

1. In your slow cooker, mix the chicken with the salsa, stock, onion and garlic powder, cilantro, oregano, paprika, salt, pepper, cumin and chili, cover, cook on Low for 7 hours, toss, divide between plates and serve with parsley sprinkled on top.

Enjoy!

Nutrition: calories 300, fat 4, fiber 7, carbs 20, protein 15

Honey Chicken Wings

You will enjoy this for sure!

Preparation time: 10 minutes

Cooking time: 6 hours

Servings: 4

Ingredients:

- 3 pounds chicken wings
- ¾ cup honey
- 1 and ½ tablespoons garlic, minced
- 2 tablespoons olive oil
- A pinch of salt and black pepper

Method:

1. In your slow cooker, mix chicken wings with garlic, oil, salt, pepper and the honey, toss well, cover, cook on Low for 6 hours, divide between plates and serve with a side salad.

Enjoy!

Nutrition: calories 261, fat 6, fiber 7, carbs 22, protein 18

Coconut Chicken Curry

This Indian dish really caught our attention!

Preparation time: 10 minutes

Cooking time: 7 hours

Servings: 4

Ingredients:

- 14 ounces coconut milk
- 3 tablespoons red curry paste
- 1 tablespoon soy sauce
- 1 tablespoon sugar
- 1 tablespoon ginger, grated
- 3 garlic cloves, minced
- 1 pound chicken thighs, skinless, boneless and cut into pieces
- 1 yellow onion, chopped
- 2 cups kale, torn

Method:

1. In your slow cooker, mix the milk with the curry paste, soy sauce, sugar, ginger, garlic and the onion and whisk.

2. Add the chicken, toss, cover, cook on Low for 6 hours and 30 minutes, add the kale, cook for 30 minutes more, divide into bowls and serve.

Enjoy!

Nutrition: calories 330, fat 11, fiber 8, carbs 22, protein 17

Shredded Chicken Mix

This is the perfect dish for a party with friends!

Preparation time: 10 minutes

Cooking time: 6 hours

Servings: 2

Ingredients:

- 2 tomatoes, roughly chopped
- 2 red onions, roughly
- 2 chicken breasts, skinless and boneless
- 2 garlic cloves, minced
- 1 tablespoon maple syrup
- 1 teaspoon chili powder
- 1 teaspoon basil, dried
- 3 tablespoons chicken stock
- 1 teaspoon cloves

Method:

1. In your slow cooker, mix the tomatoes with the onions, chicken, garlic, maple syrup, chili powder, basil and stock, cover and cook on Low for 6 hours.

2. Shred the meat, divide it and the mix from the slow cooker into bowls and serve.

Enjoy!

Nutrition: calories 281, fat 3, fiber 3, carbs 17, protein 11

Easy Chicken Thighs Mix

It's an easy mix! Try it!

Preparation time: 10 minutes

Cooking time: 6 hours

Servings: 2

Ingredients:

- 2 tablespoons tomato paste
- 1 onion, chopped
- 1 tablespoon olive oil
- Salt and black pepper to the taste
- 1 teaspoon oregano, dried
- 1 garlic clove, minced
- A pinch of red pepper flakes
- ¼ cup chicken stock
- 4 ounces canned tomatoes, chopped
- 4 chicken thighs

Method:

1. In your slow cooker, mix the tomato paste with the onion, oil, salt, pepper, oregano, garlic, pepper flakes, stock and tomatoes and stir well.

2. Add the chicken pieces, cover, cook on Low for 6 hours, toss, divide between plates and serve.

Enjoy!

Nutrition: calories 280, fat 4, fiber 6, carbs 22, protein 18

Simple Chicken

Make sure you have enough for the entire family!

Preparation time: 10 minutes

Cooking time: 6 hours

Servings: 4

Ingredients:

- 1 chicken, cut into medium pieces
- 4 thyme springs, chopped
- 2 celery stalks, chopped
- 2 garlic cloves, minced
- 1 carrot, chopped
- 1 yellow onion, chopped
- A pinch of salt and black pepper
- Juice of 1 lemon

Method:

1. In your slow cooker, mix the chicken pieces with the thyme, celery, garlic, carrot, onion, salt, pepper and the lemon juice, cover, cook on Low for 6 hours, toss, divide between plates and serve.

Enjoy!

Nutrition: calories 320, fat 4, fiber 7, carbs 22, protein 18

Chicken and Beans

This is a Mexican dish everyone needs to try!

Preparation time: 10 minutes

Cooking time: 6 hours

Servings: 2

Ingredients:

- ½ pound rotisserie chicken, shredded
- 6 ounces great northern beans, drained
- 1 garlic clove, minced
- ½ celery stalk, chopped
- 1 small yellow onion, chopped
- 1 cup chicken stock
- ½ teaspoon thyme, chopped
- ½ teaspoon sage, chopped
- ¼ teaspoon chili powder
- ¼ teaspoon smoked paprika
- A pinch of salt and black pepper

Method:

1. In your slow cooker, the chicken with the beans, garlic, celery, onion, stock, thyme, sage, chili powder, salt, pepper and the paprika, toss, cover and cook on Low for 6 hours.

2. Divide everything between plates and serve.

Enjoy!

Nutrition: calories 331, fat 6, fiber 7, carbs 27, protein 15

Pork Casserole

This is very hearty and super tasty!

Preparation time: 10 minutes

Cooking time: 6 hours

Servings: 4

Ingredients:

- 1 teaspoon lime zest, grated
- A drizzle of olive oil
- 1 pound pork, ground
- 1 tablespoon lime juice
- 1 tablespoon balsamic vinegar
- 2 garlic cloves, minced
- ½ cup yellow onion, chopped
- ½ teaspoon basil, dried
- 17 ounces mushrooms, sliced
- Salt and black pepper to the taste
- ¼ teaspoon red pepper flakes

Directions:

3. In your slow cooker, mix the oil with the lime juice, lime zest, vinegar, garlic, onion, basil, pepper flakes, salt and pepper and stir.

4. Add the pork and the mushrooms, cover, cook on Low for 6 hours, divide between plates and serve.

Enjoy!

Nutrition: calories 271, fat 6, fiber 8, carbs 18, protein 8

Balsamic Pork Shoulder Mix

This dish is extraordinaire!

Preparation time: 10 minutes

Cooking time: 7 hours

Servings: 6

Ingredients:

- 3 pounds pork shoulder
- ¼ cup balsamic vinegar
- 4 cups chicken stock
- 2 tablespoons chili sauce
- 1 tablespoon ginger, grated
- Juice of 1 lime
- 2 cups baby mushrooms, sliced
- A pinch of salt and black pepper
- 1 teaspoon cinnamon powder
- 1 tablespoon star anise seeds
- ½ teaspoons fennel seeds

Directions:

1. In your slow cooker, mix the pork with the vinegar, stock, chili sauce, ginger, lime juice, mushrooms, salt, pepper, cinnamon, star anise and fennel, cover, cook on Low for 7 hours.

2. Slice the meat, divide it between plates, add the mushrooms mix on top and serve.

Enjoy!

Nutrition: calories 362, fat 4, fiber 5, carbs 20, protein 9

Citrus Pork Loin

Just gather all your ingredients and make this tonight!

Preparation time: 10 minutes

Cooking time: 8 hours

Servings: 6

Ingredients:

- 2 pounds pork tenderloin
- 1 yellow onion, chopped
- 3 garlic cloves, minced
- 1 jalapeno, chopped
- A pinch of salt and black pepper
- Juice of 1 lime
- Juice of 1 orange
- 1 tablespoon oregano, dried
- 1 tablespoon olive oil
- 2 teaspoons cumin, ground

Directions:

1. In your slow cooker, mix the pork with the oil, onion, garlic, jalapeno, salt, pepper, lime juice, orange juice, cumin and oregano, cover, cook on Low for 8 hours, slice, divide the meat and cooking juices between plates and serve with parsley sprinkled on top.

Enjoy!

Nutrition: calories 281, fat 4, fiber 6, carbs 20, protein 18

Apple Pork

This is the right combination!

Preparation time: 10 minutes

Cooking time: 8 hours

Servings: 4

Ingredients:

- 1 pound pork tenderloin
- 2 tablespoons olive oil
- 3 apples, cored and sliced
- 1 red onion, chopped
- ½ tablespoon cinnamon powder
- A pinch of salt and black pepper

Directions:

1. In your slow cooker, mix the oil with the apples, onion, cinnamon, salt and pepper and toss.

2. Add the tenderloin on top, cover, cook on Low for 8 hours, slice the meat, divide everything between plates and serve.

Enjoy!

Nutrition: calories 320, fat 6, fiber 8, carbs 27, protein 20

Pork Chops and Peaches Mix

The pork goes really well with this sauce!

Preparation time: 10 minutes

Cooking time: 7 hours

Servings: 4

Ingredients:

- 1 teaspoon ginger, grated
- 2 garlic cloves, minced
- 1 yellow onion, chopped
- 1 and ½ cups tomato sauce
- 1 tablespoon olive oil
- 3 peaches, cut into chunks
- 2 tablespoons balsamic vinegar
- Salt and black pepper to the taste
- 4 pork chops, bone-in

Directions:

1. In your slow cooker, mix the ginger with the garlic, onion, tomato sauce, oil, peaches, vinegar, salt and pepper and whisk.

2. Add the pork, cover, cook on Low for 7 hours, slice the meat, divide it and the sauce between plates and serve.

Enjoy!

Nutrition: calories 311, fat 7, fiber 8, carbs 18, protein 11

Fruity Sausage Mix

You will like this combination for sure!

Preparation time: 10 minutes

Cooking time: 3 hours

Servings: 6

Ingredients:

- 24 ounces pork sausages, browned and sliced
- 1 yellow onion, chopped
- 4 celery ribs, chopped
- 3 tablespoons olive oil
- 1 teaspoon oregano, dried
- 1 teaspoon Italian seasoning
- 5 pears, cored and cubed
- 1 cup cranberries
- 2 cups chicken stock

Directions:

1. In your slow cooker, mix the sausage with the onion, celery, oil, oregano, Italian seasoning, pears, cranberries and the stock, cover, cook on Low for 3 hours, toss, divide between plates and serve.

Enjoy!

Nutrition: calories 192, fat 4, fiber 5, carbs 14, protein 6

Pork and Pineapple

It's really something different!

Preparation time: 10 minutes

Cooking time: 6 hours

Servings: 2

Ingredients:

- 1 pound pork chops
- 2 tablespoons sugar
- 2 tablespoons tomato paste
- 6 ounces pineapple, cubed
- 1 tablespoon balsamic vinegar
- 2 tablespoons soy sauce
- 1 teaspoon garlic, minced
- 1 tablespoon parsley, chopped

Directions:

1. In your slow cooker, mix the pork chops with the sugar, tomato paste, pineapple, vinegar, soy sauce and garlic, toss, cover, cook on Low for 6 hours, divide between plates and serve.

Enjoy!

Nutrition: calories 281, fat 5, fiber 7, carbs 19, protein 20

Pork Roast Mix

This roast is perfect when served with this next veggie mix!

Preparation time: 10 minutes

Cooking time: 8 hours

Servings: 2

Ingredients:

- ½ pound gold potatoes, chopped
- 1 pound pork roast
- 2 carrots, chopped
- 6 ounces canned tomatoes, chopped
- 1 small yellow onion, chopped
- Zest of ½ lime, grated
- Juice of ½ lime
- 2 garlic cloves, minced
- Salt and black pepper to the taste

Directions:

1. In your slow cooker, mix the potatoes with the carrots, tomatoes, onion, lime juice and zest, garlic, salt and pepper and toss.

2. Add the roast on top, cover, cook on Low for 8 hours, slice the meat divide it and the veggies between plates and serve.

Enjoy!

Nutrition: calories 360, fat 4, fiber 3, carbs 19, protein 17

Pork and Cannellini Beans Mix

This is an Italian style dish! Enjoy it!

Preparation time: 10 minutes

Cooking time: 8 hours

Servings: 2

Ingredients:

- 6 ounces canned cannellini beans, drained
- 1 small red bell pepper, chopped
- ¼ cup yellow onion, chopped
- 1 teaspoon Italian seasoning
- ½ tablespoon olive oil
- ½ pound pork loin, boneless
- Salt and black pepper to the taste
- 6 ounces canned roasted tomatoes, drained and chopped
- 1 tablespoon rosemary, chopped

Directions:

1. In your slow cooker, mix the cannellini beans with the bell pepper, Italian seasoning, oil, salt, pepper, rosemary and the tomatoes and toss.

2. Add the pork loin, toss a bit, cover, cook on Low for 8 hours, slice the meat, divide it and the mix from the pot between plates and serve.

Enjoy!

Nutrition: calories 371, fat 12, fiber 5, carbs 18, protein 29

Mixed Pork and Beef

This is perfect for a winter meal!

Preparation time: 10 minutes

Cooking time: 8 hours

Servings: 2

Ingredients:

- ½ pound black beans
- 1 bacon slice, chopped
- 1 tablespoon olive oil
- ½ pound pork shoulder, cubed
- Salt and black pepper to the taste
- ½ pound beef chuck, boneless and cut into medium cubes
- 3 garlic cloves, minced
- ½ yellow onion, chopped
- ½ cup beef stock
- ¼ tablespoon apple cider vinegar
- ½ bunch collard greens

Directions:

1. In your slow cooker, mix the beans with the bacon, oil, pork and beef cubes, salt, pepper, garlic, onion, stock and the vinegar, toss, cover, cook on Low for 7 hours and 40 minutes, add the greens, cover again and cook on Low for 20 minutes more.

2. Divide everything into bowls and serve.

Enjoy!

Nutrition: calories 361, fat 10, fiber 12, carbs 20, protein 30

Beef and Red Wine Sauce

It's such an elegant and rich dish!

Preparation time: 10 minutes

Cooking time: 8 hours

Servings: 2

Ingredients:

- ½ cup beef stock
- ½ teaspoon mustard
- 2 carrots, chopped
- 2 ounces cremini mushrooms, halved
- ½ red onion, chopped
- 1 celery rib, chopped
- 1 garlic clove, minced
- ½ tablespoon olive oil
- 1 pound beef roast, cut into medium cubes
- Salt and black pepper to the taste
- 2 tablespoons tomato paste
- ¼ cup red wine
- ½ tablespoon butter
- 1 tablespoon parsley, chopped

Directions:

1. In your slow cooker, mix the stock with the mustard, carrots, mushrooms, onion, celery, garlic, oil, salt, pepper, tomato paste, wine and butter and toss.

2. Add the beef, toss, cover, cook on Low for 8 hours, divide everything between plates and serve.

Enjoy!

Nutrition: calories 361, fat 20, fiber 4, carbs 19, protein 29

Creamy Beef and Pasta

It's time for you to try this!

Preparation time: 10 minutes

Cooking time: 8 hours

Servings: 2

Ingredients:

- 1 pound beef stew meat
- 1 teaspoon Italian seasoning
- Salt and black pepper to the taste
- 1 cup beef stock
- ½ cup mushrooms, sliced
- 1 and ½ tablespoon Worcestershire sauce
- 1 teaspoon garlic, minced
- ½ tablespoon mustard
- 1 cup sour cream
- 2 tablespoons cornstarch
- 6 ounces pasta noodles, cooked

Directions:

1. In your slow cooker, mix the beef with the seasoning, salt, pepper, stock, mushrooms, Worcestershire sauce, garlic, mustard, sour cream and cornstarch, cover, cook on Low for 8 hours, divide between plates and serve with pasta noodles on the side.

Enjoy!

Nutrition: calories 372, fat 6, fiber 9, carbs 18, protein 19

Short Ribs Delight

The name says it all!

Preparation time: 10 minutes

Cooking time: 8 hours

Servings: 2

Ingredients:

- 2 beef short ribs, bone in and cut into individual ribs
- Salt and black pepper to the taste
- ¼ cup beef stock
- ½ cup BBQ sauce
- 1 tablespoon mustard
- 1 tablespoon green onions, chopped

Directions:

1. In your slow cooker, mix the ribs with salt, pepper, BBQ sauce and the mustard, cover, cook on Low for 8 hours, toss, divide between plates and serve with the onions sprinkled on top.

Enjoy!

Nutrition: calories 264, fat 7, 4, carbs 18, protein 17

Beef Roast and Tomato Sauce

You should make this for your friends today!

Preparation time: 10 minutes

Cooking time: 6 hours

Servings: 4

Ingredients:

- 2 pounds beef roast
- 1 red chili pepper, minced
- 7 ounces tomato sauce
- 1 red onion, chopped
- 1 cup beef stock
- 2 tablespoons cumin, ground
- 2 tablespoons olive oil
- 1 tablespoon oregano, chopped
- 1 tablespoon sweet paprika
- 1 tablespoon garlic, minced
- ½ cup cilantro, chopped

Directions:

1. In your slow cooker, mix the roast with the chili pepper, tomato sauce, onion, stock, cumin, oil, oregano, paprika and garlic, cover, cook on Low for 6 hours, toss, slice the meat, divide it and the sauce between plates and serve with cilantro sprinkled on top.

Enjoy!

Nutrition: calories 371, fat 4, fiber 6, carbs 16, protein 9

Beef Roast and Soy Sauce Mix

Here's a tasty Asian style mix!

Preparation time: 10 minutes

Cooking time: 8 hours

Servings: 6

Ingredients:

- 5 pounds beef chuck roast
- 2 tablespoons Italian seasoning
- 1 cup beef stock
- 1 tablespoon soy sauce
- 10 peperoncinis
- 3 tablespoons olive oil

Directions:

1. In your slow cooker, mix the roast with the seasoning, stock, soy sauce, oil and peperoncinis, toss, cover and cook on Low for 8 hours.

2. Shred the meat, divide it and the cooking juices between plates and serve.

Enjoy!

Nutrition: calories 351, fat 5, fiber 7, carbs 20, protein 19

Beef and Cauliflower

It's a special and delicious meal!

Preparation time: 10 minutes

Cooking time: 8 hours

Servings: 4

Ingredients:

- 1 and ½ pounds beef flank steak, sliced and cubed
- 1 cup beef stock
- 2/3 cup soy sauce
- 1/3 cup sugar
- 1 tablespoon olive oil
- 1 tablespoons garlic, minced
- ¼ teaspoon chili powder
- 4 cups cauliflower florets

Directions:

1. In your slow cooker, mix the beef with the stock, soy sauce, sugar, oil, garlic, chili and cauliflower, toss, cover, cook on Low for 8 hours, divide between plates and serve.

Enjoy!

Nutrition: calories 271, fat 7, fiber 10, carbs 19, protein 16

Mexican Beef and Veggie Mix

You need to try this right now!

Preparation time: 10 minutes

Cooking time: 8 hours

Servings: 6

Ingredients:

- 2 pounds beef meat, cubed
- 1 garlic clove, minced
- 1 yellow onion, chopped
- 28 ounces canned tomato sauce
- 15 ounces canned tomatoes, chopped
- 3 cups beef stock
- 2 gold potatoes, chopped
- 4 tablespoons chili powder
- ¼ teaspoon basil, dried

Directions:

1. In your slow cooker, mix the beef with the garlic, onion, tomato sauce, tomatoes, stock, potatoes, chili powder and basil, cover, cook on Low for 8 hours, divide between plates and serve.

Enjoy!

Nutrition: calories 311, fat 7, fiber 9, carbs 20, protein 17

Simple Hungarian Beef Roast

This beef roast is absolutely incredible!

Preparation time: 10 minutes

Cooking time: 6 hours

Servings: 4

Ingredients:

- 2 pounds beef roast
- 1 chili pepper, chopped
- 7 ounces tomato sauce
- 1 yellow onion, chopped
- 1 cup beef stock
- 2 tablespoons cumin, ground
- 2 tablespoons olive oil
- 1 tablespoon oregano, chopped
- 1 tablespoon smoked paprika
- 1 tablespoon garlic, minced
- ½ cup cilantro, chopped

Directions:

2. In your slow cooker, mix the roast with the chili pepper, tomato sauce, onion, stock, cumin, oil, oregano, paprika and garlic, toss, cover and cook on Low for 6 hours.

3. Slice the roast, divide it and the cooking juices between plates, sprinkle the cilantro on top and serve.

Enjoy!

Nutrition: calories 342, fat 4, fiber 6, carbs 20, protein 15

Slow Cooked Lamb Chops Delight

This is an irresistible dish!

Preparation time: 10 minutes

Cooking time: 4 hours

Servings: 4

Ingredients:

- ½ teaspoon garlic powder
- 1 yellow onion, sliced
- 1 teaspoon oregano, dried
- ½ teaspoon thyme, dried
- A pinch of salt and black pepper
- 8 lamb loin chops
- 2 garlic cloves, minced

Method:

1. In your slow cooker, mix the garlic powder with the onion, oregano, thyme, salt, pepper, lamb chops and the garlic, toss, cover, cook on Low for 4 hours, divide between plates and serve.

Enjoy!

Nutrition: calories 200, fat 8, fiber 4, carbs 8, protein 20

Delicious Lamb Chops

This is a special dish you should try!

Preparation time: 10 minutes

Cooking time: 5 hours

Servings: 4

Ingredients:

- 1 teaspoon olive oil
- 2 pound lamb chops
- 1 red onion, sliced
- 12 ounces canned tomatoes, chopped
- 3 garlic cloves, minced
- 1 cup red wine
- 1 rosemary spring
- 4 thyme springs
- 2 ounces feta cheese, crumbled
- 1/3 cup parsley, chopped
- 2 teaspoons lemon juice
- Salt and black pepper to the taste

Method:

1. In your slow cooker, mix the oil with the lamb chops, onion, tomatoes, garlic, wine, rosemary, thyme, lemon juice, salt and pepper, cover and cook on Low for 5 hours.

2. Add the parsley and the cheese, toss a bit, leave everything aside for 10 minutes, divide between plates and serve.

Enjoy!

Nutrition: calories 291, fat 7, fiber 6, carbs 17, protein 20

Slow Cooker Dessert Recipes

We know you all love a good dessert and that's why we searched for the best slow cooked ones! They are all easy to make and you will definitely enjoy them all!

Cocoa Cake

Did you know you could make a delicious cake in your slow cooker?

Preparation time: 10 minutes

Cooking time: 3 hours

Servings: 10

Ingredients:

- 1 cup white flour
- ½ cup sugar
- ½ cup cocoa powder
- 1 and ½ teaspoons baking powder
- 3 eggs
- 2 tablespoons canola oil
- 2/3 cup milk
- 1 teaspoon vanilla extract
- Cooking spray

Directions:

1. In a bowl, mix the flour with the cocoa, sugar, baking powder, eggs, oil, milk and vanilla and whisk really well.

2. Pour this into your slow cooker greased with cooking spray, spread, cover, cook on High for 3 hours, slice, divide between plates and serve.

Enjoy!

Nutrition: calories 231, fat 11, fiber 5, carbs 14, protein 8

Simple Cinnamon Apple Mix

This fall dessert is so tasty!

Preparation time: 10 minutes

Cooking time: 3 hours

Servings: 4

Ingredients:

- 8 apples, cored, peeled and sliced
- 3 tablespoons sugar
- 1 tablespoons lime juice
- 1 teaspoon cinnamon powder
- 2 tablespoons canola oil

Directions:

1. In your slow cooker, mi the apple slices with the sugar, lime juice, cinnamon and the oil, toss, cover, cook on High for 3 hours, divide between plates and serve cold.

Enjoy!

Nutrition: calories 191, fat 4, fiber 7, carbs 9, protein 9

Apples and Rose Water Mix

The flavor is insane!

Preparation time: 10 minutes

Cooking time: 3 hours

Servings: 4

Ingredients:

- 4 apples, cored
- 4 tablespoons rose water
- 3 tablespoons sugar

Directions:

1. In your slow cooker, mix the apples with the rose water and sugar, cover, cook on High for 3 hours, divide between plates and serve.

Enjoy!

Nutrition: calories 260, fat 4, fiber 6, carbs 11, protein 7

Lemony Bars

These bars taste so fresh! Try them!

Preparation time: 10 minutes

Cooking time: 2 hours and 30 minutes

Servings: 8

Ingredients:

- 12 tablespoons butter, soft
- 1 teaspoon vanilla extract
- 1 cup sugar
- 1 egg
- 2 cups white flour
- 10 ounces lemon curd
- Cooking spray

Directions:

1. In your slow cooker, mix the butter with the vanilla, sugar, egg, flour and lemon curd and stir well until you obtain a smooth batter.

2. Grease your slow cooker with the cooking spray, add the batter, spread, cover, cook on High for 2 hours and 30 minutes, leave aside to cool down, slice and serve as a dessert.

Enjoy!

Nutrition: calories 191, fat 12, fiber 5, carbs 12, protein 6

Cinnamon Banana Mix

Serve this for your friends today!

Preparation time: 10 minutes

Cooking time: 2 hours

Servings: 4

Ingredients:

- 8 bananas, peeled and sliced
- 1 cup coconut flakes
- 1 teaspoon cinnamon powder
- ¼ cup honey
- ½ cup canola oil
- 1 teaspoon vanilla extract
- ¼ cup lime juice
- 2 teaspoons lime zest, grated

Directions:

In your slow cooker, mix the bananas with the coconut flakes, cinnamon, honey, oil, vanilla, lime zest and lime juice, cover, cook on Low for 2 hours, divide into bowls and serve cold.

Nutrition: calories 179, fat 4, fiber 7, carbs 11, protein 5

Coconut Pear Mix

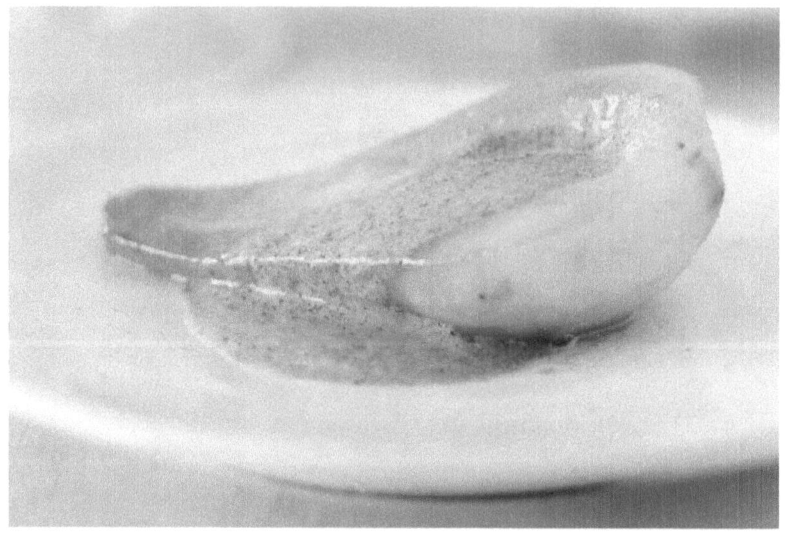

It's something different and so rich!

Preparation time: 10 minutes

Cooking time: 4 hours

Servings: 8

Ingredients:

- 8 pears, cored and sliced
- ½ cup raisins
- ¼ cup coconut milk
- 1 teaspoon ginger, grated
- ¼ cup sugar
- 1 teaspoon lime zest, grated

Directions:

1. In your slow cooker, mix the pears with the raisins, milk, ginger, sugar and lime zest, cover, cook on Low for 4 hours, toss, divide into bowls and serve.

Enjoy!

Nutrition: calories 181, fat 3, fiber 4, carbs 13, protein 6

Great Apple Mix

This apple stew is so good! Taste it and see!

Preparation time: 10 minutes

Cooking time: 4 hours

Servings: 8

Ingredients:

- 2 tablespoons lime juice
- 2 pounds apples, cored, peeled and cubed
- 4 cups sugar
- 1 teaspoon cinnamon powder
- 1 teaspoon vanilla extract

Directions:

1. In your slow cooker, mix the apples with lime juice, sugar, cinnamon and vanilla, cover, cook on Low for 4 hours, toss, divide into ramekins and serve warm.

Enjoy!

Nutrition: calories 180, fat 4, fiber 6, carbs 11, protein 5

Coconut Cream

You only need 3 ingredients to make this tasty dessert!

Preparation time: 10 minutes

Cooking time: 1 hour

Servings: 2

Ingredients:

- 2 ounces coconut cream
- 2 ounces dark chocolate, cut into chunks
- 1 teaspoon sugar

Directions:

1. In your slow cooker, mix the chocolate and the coconut cream and sugar, whisk, cover, cook on High for 1 hour, whisk again, divide into bowls and serve cold.

Enjoy!

Nutrition: calories 222, fat 6, fiber 6, carbs 9, protein 6

Cherry Compote

Here's a spring dessert everyone loves!

Preparation time: 10 minutes

Cooking time: 2 hours

Servings: 2

Ingredients:

- ¼ cup cocoa powder
- ½ cup red cherry juice
- 2 tablespoons maple syrup
- ½ pound cherries, pitted and halved
- 1 tablespoons sugar
- 2 cups water

Directions:

1. In your slow cooker, mix the cherries with the sugar, water, cherry juice, cocoa and maple syrup, cover, cook on High for 2 hours, toss, divide into bowls and serve cold.

Enjoy!

Nutrition: calories 190, fat 1, fiber 4, carbs 7, protein 6

Plum Compote

How can you not try this?

Preparation time: 10 minutes

Cooking time: 1 hour and 30 minutes

Servings: 2

Ingredients:

- 1 pound plums, stones removed and sliced
- 1 cup water
- 1 tablespoon sugar

Directions:

1. In your slow cooker, mix the plums with the sugar and water, cover, cook on High for 1 hour and 30 minutes, toss, divide into bowls and serve.

Enjoy!

Nutrition: calories 183, fat 1, fiber 1, carbs 6, protein 5

Conclusion

The slow cooker recipes collection you've just discovered is pretty impressive. We gathered some of the best slow cooker recipes just for you. These recipes are all incredible and they will gain your hearts forever.

The recipes we collected for you are all easy to make at home if you have your slow cooker at hand. These dishes are so rich, flavored and delicious and everyone will love them for sure,

All in all, this special collection is awesome and it you should get your hands on a copy as soon as possible.

So, what are you waiting for? opt for this slow cooker collection right away and start cooking in a different, new and original way.

Slow cooking is an incredible cooking method and it will totally surprise you.

Have fun in the kitchen and enjoy.

Dear Reader,

Thank you very much for choosing my book. I hope you really enjoy it. If don't mind I would like to ask you to leave a review after reading.

Thanks.

Sincerely yours,

Stephanie Sharp